GARY COOPER
OFF CAMERA

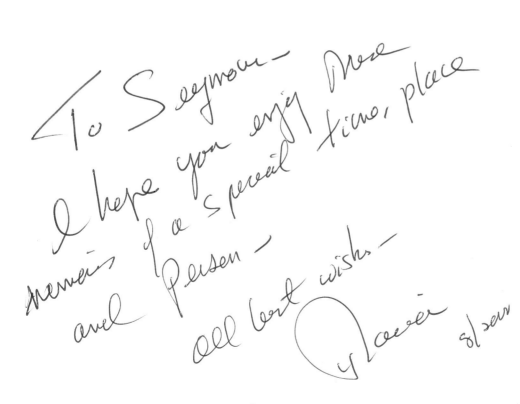

To Seymour—
I hope you enjoy these
memories of a special time, place
and Person—
all best wishes—
Maria
8/2011

GARY COOPER OFF CAMERA

A Daughter Remembers

Maria Cooper Janis

with an introduction by
Tom Hanks

HARRY N. ABRAMS, INC., PUBLISHERS

EDITOR: Ruth A. Peltason
DESIGNER: Raymond P. Hooper

Page 2: Gary Cooper crossing stream, Sun Valley, 1940. (Photograph, Robert Capa); page 5 (clockwise from top): Gary Cooper stunt riding, c. 1938; Gary Cooper, Ernest Hemingway, 1940. (Photograph, Lloyd Arnold); Gary Cooper, Aspen; Gary and Maria Cooper, 1958; Gary and Rocky Cooper, 1933; Gary and Maria Cooper looking out at the Grand Canyon.

Library of Congress Cataloging-in-Publication Data

Janis, Maria Cooper.
    Gary Cooper off camera : a daughter remembers / Maria Cooper Janis ; with an introduction by Tom Hanks.
        p.   cm.
    ISBN 0–8109–4130–9
    1. Cooper, Gary, 1901–1961.   2. Janis, Maria Cooper.   3. Motion picture actors and actresses—United States—Biography.   I. Title.
PN2287.C59J36   1999
791.43'028'092—dc21
[B]   99–13833

Printed and bound in Japan

HARRY N. ABRAMS, INC,
100 FIFTH AVENUE
NEW YORK, N.Y. 10011
www.abramsbooks.com

Contents

Introduction

by Tom Hanks

If there is any question as to whether a larger-than-life movie star can also be an artist of great mystery, consider the life and work of Gary Cooper, particularly the final fourteen minutes of High Noon in which Cooper delivers only seven words of scripted dialogue.

Since *High Noon* is arguably one of the greatest motion pictures of all time and his performance as Will Kane earned Cooper his second Academy Award, one would think these seven words would be remembered as among the most notable and repeated in all of movie history. But since this is *High Noon* and the actor is Gary Cooper, the lines "Miller!" and "I'll come out. Let her go" are only words of dialogue and no threat to the likes of "Here's looking at you, kid," or "Frankly, Scarlett, I don't give a damn."

The emotional impact of Stanley Kramer's production springs from the film's silent moments, certainly from the direction of Fred Zinnemann and the editing of Elmo Williams and Harry Gerstad. And, of course, from the looks, gestures, and reactions found in the performance of the film's star. He strides up the streets of Hadleyville, flicks sweat from his brow as he stands alone in the center of the suddenly deserted town, looks on in emotional pain as both his new wife and his old flame abandon him. Gary Cooper is not just Sheriff Will Kane in *High Noon*—he is also a mysterious and cryptic teacher of the art of acting on the screen. The kind of teacher who confounds and inspires his students at the same time—a professional duty he began, appropriately enough, in the era of silent motion pictures.

In only one scene in the first film to win the Academy Award for Best Picture, *Wings,* we see the future of screen acting in the form of Gary Cooper. He is quiet and natural, somehow different from the other famous cast members. He does something mysterious with his eyes and shoulders that is much more like "being" than "acting." He does nothing that telegraphs to the audience his process. And yet, there is some kind of process there, for the man is "acting." He is in a costume and makeup. He is standing in front of not only a camera, but also the multitude of people who made up a film crew even when films were silent. In this one scene, Cooper somehow crosses a bridge from the artifice of acting to the manner of behavior via a process that eludes most other performers—a process that marks the difference between a popular film star and untouchable film icon years ahead of his time.

It is not hard to presume that the advent of sound in film made not a dent in his way of working—in his process—for as shown in the great majority of his film roles Cooper could have coined and patented the phrase "less is more." Remember that at the height of his celebrity, in all the cartoon caricatures and imitations, all that was required to satirize Gary Cooper was a quiet "Yup."

At the same time as he was the man of few words in the Hollywood firmament, Cooper was, like all movie stars, churning out films at a dizzying pace compared to today's production schedules. His output for 1940–1942 began with *North West Mounted Police,* directed by Cecil B. DeMille. Then, in succession, Cooper starred in Capra's *Meet John Doe,* Howard Hawks's *Sergeant York* (for which he won his first Best Actor Academy Award) and *Ball of Fire,* as Lou Gehrig in Sam Wood's *The Pride of the Yankees,* and finally in *For Whom the Bell Tolls* (released in 1943). All the big stars and contract players of the era worked at this voluminous pace. In fact, during this incredible run of films Cooper co-starred twice with Barbara Stanwyck, the actress who could easily be considered his female counterpart.

The number of movies is not so impressive as the impact each had on the movie audience. *North West Mounted Police* is not considered a great classic, but *Meet John Doe* certainly is. As the title character in *Sergeant York,* Cooper touched an American nerve, making the film the top-grossing picture of the year. Then, in *Ball of Fire,* Cooper appeared in as delightful a film of the era as one will find.

Cooper again entered the consciousness of the nation with *The Pride of the Yankees,* a film of such timely perfection that it even features Babe Ruth. The moving final speech of Lou Gehrig—"I consider myself the luckiest man on the face of the earth"—has since become a *gestalt* quotation now used at almost any occasion. During World War II, Cooper recited the speech for GI's during USO tours in the South Pacific. Finally, Ernest Hemingway himself wanted Cooper to play Robert Jordan in *For Whom the Bell Tolls,* earning the actor his fourth Academy Award nomination.

There is not an actor alive who would not give his all to have just one of these film roles as a credit. Two would make a career. But to turn in five of these performances in a row requires an actor with the presence, process, and simple yet mysterious star quality of a Gary Cooper.

Of course, not all the years were as good for Cooper as those of the early forties. The year 1933 found Cooper appearing in such forgotten films as *Design for Living, Alice in Wonderland* (look it up!), and *Operator 13,* in 1934. But even the lesser films of his career only enhance the mystery of Gary Cooper and his process. Was acting in films really as easy for him as he made it look? Did he simply hit his marks and do what came naturally? Did he ever have any difficulty overcoming the self-consciousness that is part and parcel of standing in front of a camera while pretending to be Lou Gehrig, Alvin York, or Will Kane?

Perhaps we will never know. Looking to the man himself for some hint will turn up precious few clues. There is an old story in Hollywood about Cooper on the set of one of his films, which could very well have been *High Noon.* Between shots, the other cast members were passing the time, talking as all actors do about their roles, their lines, and the merits of one script over another. Hoping to include the great star in conversation, one of the actors asked, "Mr. Cooper, what are the things you look for in a script?"

Without looking up, the cryptic yet larger-than-life professor of the Gary Cooper School of the Art of Screen Acting gave a simple lesson.

"Days off," he said.

Letter to My Father

Dear Poppa,

I want your friends and fans to know how it was, to know how you were. It's many years past, but it's also that funny place of mind where yesterday is no more than twenty-four hours ago, and fifty—forty—thirty years ago are not separated or peeled off from today, but only part of a large meadow where from my present corner I look around and see you traipsing through the sagebrush and rocks of the Valley of the Moon, the lava flow down in the low country near Sun Valley. In another, if I squint and focus my eyes I can see you, distant but there.

More memories come, and like a cloud of ducks filling the early morning sky I point my mind at them and try to shoot—not to kill but to catch, to tame, to preserve the images of your hours spent patient and cold in a duck blind in Idaho; of your bringing home the bounty from your 4:00 A.M. sojourn to the wilds of Point Magoo; of your depositing a brace of ducks on the kitchen table before breakfast, asking the cook to feather and clean them—and her roaring in tears to my mother's room, announcing she was quitting, she was *not* engaged to clean blood and guts and feathers.

You hunted a lot. You always loved that challenge, "bred in the bone," I think, of Man versus Nature—not only as an antagonist, but in the natural order of things. You eliminated quite a few varmints. Your constant pleasure was in honing your eye, fine-tuning your gun with its telescopic lens, and your own almost Zen-like relation to the entire act of shooting.

Drawing of an eagle from Frank James (later Gary) Cooper's high school notebook.

I hear your voice telling me how to squeeze a trigger, "You don't pull the trigger, it pulls you."

My mother and I hated the killing of anything. For you, it was a natural part of growing up in Montana, the "West" of 1901–1916. Hunting was a relationship in which man stalking animal, for food or pelt, was the natural order of things. No one thought about endangered species then, but I remember your four-letter words addressed to the "sportsmen" who shot their game with a gun ten times too powerful, or those "big men" who hunted the wolf from low-flying airplanes. Your disdain for them was withering. I remember the look in your eye as you spoke of them. They were beneath contempt. Those were some of the rare times I ever saw you get angry.

But I often saw you enjoy the color of the Pacific on those mornings we would all drive down to the beach and walk, play, sleep, swim, look for little crabs scuttling to their sand caves nestled in the rocks when the tide went out; our games of who could step on the most seaweed sacs with that satisfactory "pop!" breaking an air sac like bubble paper.

Nature at her most benign touched us every day, and we went out to explore her and embrace her mysteries. "Sit still and watch, look, be aware," you said, "and you will learn many things."

You taught more by example or encouraging observation, rather than with words. To study flight, we'd go to the beach or the desert and watch the birds soar—riding air currents—catching the thermals and climbing hundreds of feet spiraling upward without having to move their wings once. You could draw birds' wings, analyze the way they were put together feather by feather. This was the best school of all—play—and there was lots of it, together as a family, part of a bigger thing. It was part of life—lessons without being *lessons*. The pieces of the world morphed into ever larger, more meaningful, chunks; and the patterns of my days fell into rhythms that gave security, depth, wonder, and joy.

Sometimes at night in now-infamous Brentwood, when the air was fragrant with jacaranda, eucalyptus, and orange blossoms, we would all stand outside quietly. You would make a series of strange sounds in your throat—a call—and usually from a distance there would be a response, far away at first, but then we would hear it coming closer and closer through the night. You had called in an owl, and I remember thinking, How beautiful that man can really talk to wild creatures.

I remember Charlie, a baby crow you found injured and brought home. You made a little leather harness for his leg and we kept him on a long tether in my enclosed garden so the dogs couldn't get to him. Eventually Charlie grew very tame and would sit on our shoulders and talk back if you spoke to him. The time came to teach him how to be free. Poppa, first you plucked the pinion feathers so he couldn't fly far until we saw that he had learned how to kill food and fend for himself. Then he began making longer flights, but wherever he was nesting (now out of sight), if we would call, he'd answer and come swooping in with a kind of glee, to land again on our shoulders or walk around our feet, talking his head off. And then that sad, sweet day—Charlie must have found a Mrs. Charlie because he didn't return.

Despite our very elaborate life, "glamorous and high powered," everything also had an extraordinary simplicity. Ours was a large and inclusive playground but in spite of the hurricanes of living, our compass always returned to a *true North.*

The contrasts within you, in retrospect, were huge, and gave our life such a diverse palette. Your mind was open to so many things. You accepted life in all its hues and colors. In fact, you sought it out.

You taught me how good-tasting beef jerky could be and sandwiches stuffed with raw sliced Bermuda onions and Hellman's mayonnaise—a feast as we drove across the desert and mountains, going to or returning from Sun Valley or Aspen. They were two places in particular that you loved, and where we spent as much time as your film schedule allowed. The need to be alone or get out with the guys, driving around the low country, "Where the coyotes howl and the wind blows free," was life's blood to you. And you loved stopping in small towns in the middle of nowhere, lunching in a dinette with your hunting buddies.

When we went to Europe, cuisine escalated to finer fare. Three dozen fresh oysters at one sitting, a fine French wine, escargots, and champagne. You name it, you loved to eat it, from chocolate soufflé to scrambled eggs smothered with jalapeño chili peppers.

You in the kitchen whipping up buttermilk hotcakes and bacon—early morning rituals that gave an "all's right with the world" feeling.

Poppa, you showed me the way arrowheads with the notch carved at the bottom fit into sticks and become spears. You drew pictures—of ancient peoples hunting, sea gulls flying, fish jumping at the end of a line, galloping horses snorting with energy and their own wildness—that excited my imagination and infused me with a love of creating my own images. You taught me that the universe is ours to make, to shape as we wish, to set the whole thing ringing. This was one of the great gifts you gave me.

There are memories too of three rings from the bedroom, telling me that you were awake, and so I would charge to the other end of the house and dive into bed between you and Momma. Those moments created a sense of protection, strength, and love beyond description. Sometimes you both would tickle me, and of course I'd tickle back. So the day started with whoops of laughter and hugging as we bounced the morning into high gear.

A special book came out in 1956 that captivated us because it put into words and images exactly what you had always done naturally, which was to explore and understand nature. The small book was titled *A Sense of Wonder*, with text by Rachel Carson, and beautiful photographs by Charles Pratt and others. It was a sheer celebration of the joy of discovering the joys of life.

You taught me how to use all my senses in discovering the songs that nature was constantly singing. I remember: being hauled out of bed at 2:00 A.M. when the three of us would lie on the grass and look into the sky at meteor showers, with the heavens raining light. You would describe celestial distances, and somehow the concept of light-years and the vastness of space was something that became real, like a breaking wave or smelling a gardenia. And I remember going to the beach during a full moon to see the grunion run, millions of little fish coming up on the sand to spawn, coating the beach in shimmering, undulating silver.

When I entered the scene, you had been on a journey with my mother for four years. Outside our home, Hollywood life consisted of idols, myths, icons and fantasy, fame, exaggeration, and hyperbole. But inside the gardens and walls of our home, we lived with fun, discipline, honor, curiosity, enthusiasm, and—always that key ingredient—love.

Nobody was a monk or the Virgin Mary in our household, but you and Momma had the bigness of spirit to let me see that you were human, two adults. You did not put yourselves on pedestals for my benefit. There was an unusual understanding of the human condition that did not seek to justify what your activities may have been, or glamorize them.

As a result, I saw the pain life caused both of you. Along with the "highs" of a new romance, the struggle to be happy was more than that, as each of you needed to fill the insecurity of your respective selves.

"Gary Cooper—insecure?" readers might gasp. Well, why not? For balance there was Rocky—Mother—the woman described by some as "being able to run the Pentagon," who was basically timid. To walk with you through the dining room at Romanoff's or at Chasen's made Momma want to crumble away and vanish, like a pulverized leaf in a wind. But to hide it—of course—Momma would toss her beautiful hair and stride into the lions' den, maybe shaking inside like a scared rabbit, wary of the predators hoping to grab you away from her. But you both kept private matters basically private, and she discreetly knew how to fight fire with fire.

Acting isn't so bad as long as you always know the difference, and can drop the act or mask at will.

In Native American (Kiowa) writer and poet Scott Momaday's book *The Man Made of Words*, he says, "To encounter the sacred is to be alive at the deepest center of human existence." Without ever using the word *sacred*, you taught me that the world is imbued with mystery and, yes, sacredness. With your love and respect of nature and your artist's eye, you showed me that mystery.

Although Lady Luck was the first of many friendly females to cross your path, you never stopped referring to yourself as "Mr. Average Joe American," and this was not an affectation. You felt this to your core, along with deep feelings of responsibility and gratitude for all your good fortune.

If you're reading this over my shoulder, I hope I present that special life we all lived in a true way. And as I write this paragraph from a plane at 30,000 feet and enjoy one of your favorite pastimes in the air, musing at the view of our earth shifting below us, I feel my own delight and wonder, as did you, with the miracle of it all.

Maria Cooper Janis
November 1998

Early Time

I would like my father's own voice to speak. Why not? He chose his words carefully in life and I would not want to put false ones in his mouth, based on my own guesses and the distortions of time.

My father's wish to be an artist goes back a long way. His interest in art was sparked around the age of nine by an encounter with a well-known mural painted by Charles M. Russell that hung in the Montana state capitol building. Here's how my father described first seeing this mural: "I had gone down to the Montana State Capitol where Dad was a judge of the Supreme Court. Halfway through the great hall I was stopped, really nailed in my tracks, by the sight of a great mural. It showed explorers, Indians and horses, and every one of them seemed ready to pick right up and move past me. I was looking at Charles Russell's painting of Lewis and Clark at Ross Hole. Years later I discovered that the mural is one of Russell's masterpieces but all I knew then, as a youngster, was that I'd give anything to be able to paint like that." Late in life my father revisited Russell's mural, painted 1911.

My father wasn't able to dive into the painting part of his life right away. Regular school took precedence, and then came the war, which called his older brother Arthur off to the fight and sent my father back to the ranch to help his mother handle five hundred

The West—Helena, Montana, 1901—
an ideal place for Frank James (Gary) Cooper to be born. My father made this sketch in 1915.

head of cattle. "It was really glamorous," he used to say, "up at four-thirty A.M. shoveling manure at forty degrees below zero."

He talked about those days and how in that time period something happened that probably altered his life permanently. He took some special art courses at Wesleyan, where he met Harvey Markham, who became one of his best friends.

"Harvey had been hit with polio as a youngster, and left with paralyzed legs. His dad had fixed him up with a special Model T Ford he could control with his hands, and he became a very good driver. Each morning Harvey would pick me up and drive me to school. Helena is not exactly a flat town, and on this particular morning we were on the way down the steepest hill when Harvey applied the hand brakes. They didn't hold. Then he grabbed the two levers controlling the foot brake and the reverse pedal. They came off in his hand. I don't know how fast we were going when we hit the corner at the bottom of the hill. We almost had it made when the front wheels jack knifed. The car just flipped. Harvey went through the canvas top on one side, and I went through on the other. Harvey was thrown clear and not damaged too much. I rolled on the ground while the car stood on its nose, and then the car rolled on me.

"We didn't have an X-ray machine, but the best

doctors in town went over me and could find no broken bones. 'Some torn ligaments in the hip,' they said. 'Just stay in bed, and time will heal this.' But I couldn't stay in bed. I was so restless that finally the doctors let me go up to the ranch for my convalescence. When hobbling on crutches became too painful, I eased around on a gentle colt. The doctors were all horsemen themselves, and they saw nothing in riding that might harm torn ligaments.

"My hip hurt me considerably, so I really learned how to ride. Up to then I had been a slam-bang, rodeo-type rider who could stick on anything that bucked, and I could punish the saddle for hours at a time. Now, with my hip hurting me, I learned to anticipate the horse's next move, and then his next, until I got to the point where I could ride at a full gallop and instinctively know just about every step and twist that horse was going to make in the next hundred yards. Every time I was caught by surprise, a sharp twinge would strike my hip, something like the jab of a knife followed by a bolt of lightning, and I would settle down to the business of watching my horse again. After a few weeks of this kind of coaching, I was riding with an ease that no amount of training could have given me.

"What was really important to me was that I had days and weeks to myself. No one expected me to work. I could read, or draw, or paint, or just go off by myself. After a long ride in the mountains, moving around was painful, so I would sit quietly. After a while the deer would come out, and rabbits, skunks, quail, ptarmigan. I read by the hour, I sketched by the hour, and sometimes I just watched and thought

At a picnic with family and friends, Montana, 1909. My father is the smaller of the two boys in overalls in the front row.

by the hour.

"By the time I was walking straight again, my mind was made up. I would finish my schooling somewhere in the East, go on to study art in Chicago, and then become a painter of nature, using a style that would fall somewhere between the detail of Audubon and the scope of Russell. So that is what I started out to be.

"Some years later, I had taken the usual bad spill for the cameras. The bone specialist came by with his report and X-rays.

"'H'm'm,' he said. 'When did you break your hip?'

"'Never did,' I said.

"He held up an X-ray plate of my hip showing a white crack going through it, looking like the Grand Canyon. 'A bad break,' he said. 'Not so much knitted together as filled in. Looks like you got it when you were a kid. What happened?'

"I told him a car crash had torn some ligaments, but when I came to the part about going horseback riding after the spill, his eyes popped. 'I don't get it,' he kept saying. 'I don't get it. You had a major break and you went horseback riding, and you kept opening the crack wider and wider. It's a wonder you didn't fall through it. Today we would put you in traction and immobilize you for weeks.'

"But suppose I had been put in traction. Where would I have learned to ride with ease? Where would I have got those weeks in the wilderness, the time to read and paint, and the time to form ambition? There is a lot of talk about 'getting the breaks' in the movies, but that busted hip of mine is the truest example I know of."

Before he was Gary, Frank Cooper, the tall "actor" second
from left, played Gibson in the Gallatin County High School
senior class production of *The Gibson Upright,* by Booth
Tarkington and Harry Don Wilson. The time was May 1922. It's
amazing what a hair style can do for you—or not!

Coop's love of Indians started early and carried through all his life. As kids, Indians were his pals. In this picture he's wearing vest and pants that he made himself. He probably made the moccasins and warbonnet, too. I still have the footgear he made for me as well as my proud possession, a junior-size warbonnet, that I remember watching him create.

It's a good way to learn patience, watching the slow preparation of the feathers, a delicate artist's hand wrapping each staff in red felt, binding it with linguine-size leather thongs, sewing and weaving the entire assemblage of feathers into a glorious crown. When you wear it and stand tall you can feel the spirit of this incredible bird stream through your entire body. I could understand why the eagle feather is sacred in the Indian tradition. Perhaps it should be in ours.

Returning from Europe in April 1932,
my father brought a new little friend that he is
introducing to his mother, Alice.

Private Time

The year is 1934, the place is Hollywood, and the woman is newlywed Veronica Cooper.

Privacy, often taken for granted, becomes a cherished commodity for any public or known figure and their family. However, one walks a fine line between being grateful that your public gives a damn and wants to see you or know about you in the first place, and being devoured by some insatiable appetite that fans and media can generate. My father gracefully and deftly handled that to perfection, I think, because he genuinely liked people—his fans—and did not think of himself as "The Star." It was never "Us" and "the others."

But our family privacy was very much protected by my mother and father—home was rarely photographed, especially when I was young. Our house was on the Movie Star Home Bus Tour route, and we knew when to lie low to avoid pulling out of the driveway into a caravan of strangers with cameras. For the most part people respected our privacy. The big redwood front gates were always open, and the more aggressive souls who would try to wander in through the back garden gate were quickly but politely escorted out by the chauffeur or gardener. There was no bodyguard business for stars in those days. Some of the Brentwood community even left their front doors unlocked. It was not a paparazzi mentality then, and I have to think that since my father treated photographers and journalists with respect they returned the favor.

Veronica (Rocky)

My mother's early childhood was colored by a difficult family situation. My grandmother, Veronica Gibbons Balfe, took off for Paris to get a divorce, taking my mother and Elvira Borg, her nanny, with her. In those days, women didn't take the bull by the horns like that very often, and the Balfe family, owner of, among other things, Austen Nichols Dry Goods and later Liquor Stores, were not happy.

My mother kept in touch with her grandfather, who owned a ranch in California, but she didn't see her own father, Harry, until a few years before his death in the late 1950s. Her Gibson Girl beautiful mother met and married Paul Shields, the successful Wall Street financier who started the brokerage house of Shields and Company. So as their newlywed life was rather full, and Miss Bennett's School for Girls was not the high point in my mother's young life (her interests ran to sports and the New York Rangers), she really couldn't wait to do something independent and different.

On Thanksgiving of 1930, my mother went to California to stay with her uncle, Cedric Gibbons, who was the art director of MGM, and his wife, the glamorous actress Delores Del Rio. She flirted briefly with the idea of a film career, but quickly decided it was not for her. Even then my mother was a woman who knew her own mind, and she always said that meeting my father spared her an embarrassing exit from the acting scene.

She made quite a mark on another scene, however. Strong and beautiful, "Rocky"—the nickname she called herself when little, which stuck—was thrown into a challenging role. To be Mrs. Gary Cooper was hard for someone as shy as she. Lots of jealousy around, particularly when your husband is the "most wanted" man in the country. Not easy, but she met it all head-on, always with her direct gaze and word. You might not like to hear it, but you knew where you stood with my mother at all times.

She and her mother, Veronica, were extremely close, and wrote each other daily. The bureau in my mother's bedroom still bursts with their letters, and reading them today, sixty years later, is like having the two of them talk to me about what happened last week. The dinner party with Paul Shields and Averell and Marie Harriman; the Shieldses buying a beautiful new painting; the cost of lamb chops; a lovely new sweater at Bergdorf Goodman's that my grandmother couldn't resist buying (with an identical one for Rocky); the trials of the dog-show circuit with their Sealyhams; buying a new puppy; tennis matches at the Meadow Club; and Paul's latest Wall Street venture.

Rocky always had a classic sense of style and chic, innately and from her mother, who would have been quite an artist if she had been career-minded. My mother's athletic prowess and love of all sports led her to tackle any physical challenge with gusto and verve. She had a vivid imagination and applied it to everything.

This very shy girl from the East Coast shone in her own right once in California, and indeed won the Man from the West, as she made their life together amusing, interesting, and fun.

Glamour as only Hurrell and Hollywood could dish up.
My mother as Sandra Shaw—her stage name—1935.

Jean Howard captured a side of my mother that most people never saw, taken under
the weeping willow tree by the pool in our garden. Rocky let the camera see inside her heart.
This is the picture of her that my father carried in his wallet.

Sandra Shaw sleepwalks in one of her only two films. In the second, *King Kong*, she is the girl who screams from the window of the Empire State Building. She claims she was so bad they even had to dub her scream.

Don't get at the wrong end of my mother's gun! She had a favorite they called "Old Betsy," a Browning 12-gauge with a compensator. She was quick and accurate—in 1939 she shot 184 straight clay pigeons to become California State Women's Skeet Champion that year. Robert Capa took this picture of my mother in Sun Valley.

The glamorous Mrs. Gary Cooper—quite a contrast to being a marksman!

Lover, Wife, Friend

Santa Monica, 1934.

LEFT: Here was an easy role for the newlywed—the wife as artist's model, Van Nuys, 1934. My father did his best to make time to keep his sketching hand in practice.

OPPOSITE: Two lovers in each other's arms with the sea as their backdrop, 1934. My parents met on Richard Barthelmes's boat bound for Catalina Island. Rocky was not like the other women Gary had known up until then. She came from a very different world and her mother was horrified at the thought that there might be an "actor" in the family. But my father soon charmed both women, really won them over. Rocky touched him in places that all the glamorous, lusty friends of his bachelorhood did not.

"Never marry an heiress or an actress," he would say, and then laugh. He didn't—he married a soulmate.

This 1937 aerial view of the house my parents built in Brentwood doesn't even begin to show all the wonderful hiding places and mysterious nooks and crannies made for childhood adventures. The dog kennels are on the right, in the middle of an orchard full of orange, grapefruit, and avocado trees. My father planted rows of corn, spaced to feed us over the entire season, and we had a chicken coop full of Bantam hens and a duck pond. Pomegranate and persimmon trees shaded the little garden outside my mother's bedroom. We even had a sort of tropical garden filled with huge banana plants.

To the left of the house stands the mulberry tree, under which my friends and I danced and played, and the tennis court. Papa's gun room was linked to the garage, the long white building on the left. And a white curved fence enclosed the private garden off my bedroom.

This was a house that protected the family and its dreams. One day when horseback riding and picnicking in a meadow high in the Santa Monica hills, my mother and father saw two beautiful oak trees. They had them transplanted to their new house, where the trees grew to enormous size. In time, they shaded the master bedroom and dining room, and I always knew their presence had a special meaning.

TOP LEFT: Relaxing at home, circa 1940. (Photograph, Maurice Terrell)

TOP RIGHT: On the town, mid-1950s.

LEFT: Momma puts a finishing touch on Poppa's kerchief, Aspen, early 1950s.

Who says dogs don't make good cargo?
My parents canoeing in Lake Tahoe, 1936.

Proud parents—of Sealyham pups, in 1936.
My parents bred and raised Sealyhams before I came along.

Rocky was a great shot. She would never kill anything, but blew the men away on the skeet field.

OPPOSITE: In those days when the hills and beaches still were accessible, my parents would "get out of Dodge"—to the quiet, or riding in the surf, or picnicking in the virgin hills above Malibu. (Photograph, Alexander Paal, 1938)

A happy father and his baby girl, 1938.

An Only Daughter Remembers

What does a father tell a daughter that is the most helpful—about life, men, sex, loving? This quote from Albert Einstein embodies one of the gifts my father gave me: "The most beautiful and most profound emotion we can experience is the sensation of the mystical. It is the source of all true science. He to whom this emotion is a stranger, who can no longer wonder and stand rapt in awe, is as good as dead. To know that what is impenetrable to us really exists, manifesting itself as the highest wisdom and the most radiant beauty which our dull faculties can comprehend only in their most primitive forms—this knowledge, this feeling, is at the center of true religiousness." Lessons about the practical side of life were never omitted, either.

Growing up with my mother was rich with talk—

With my father on top of Baldy Mountain, Sun Valley, early 1940s. (Photograph, Robert Capa)

real communication between parent and child about anything and everything. There were no subjects we couldn't and didn't discuss.

My parents (for a very creative dynamic was in motion between my mother and father) opened my awareness from day one. The following photos are a little look inside our daily life, but what informed that life was the living out of those ideas that Albert Einstein expressed so beautifully.

My father was always teaching me how to *look far* (and underfoot too), in this case at the Grand Canyon.

A late afternoon hug in our library in Brentwood—
my buckskin jacket was handmade by my father. On
the desk, next to his first Oscar, sits a bazooka
brought back from the South Pacific. (Photograph,
Maurice Terrell)

Our wonderful grapefruit-eating boxer, Arno,
tries to plant a sloppy kiss on my father's chin, around
1945. (Photograph, Inga Arvad)

OPPOSITE: Poppa and me leaving Sun Valley Lodge to catch a bus ride to the bottom of Baldy Mountain, 1948.

TOP: What accuracy! But then he was a willing stationary target, and I was awfully close. Aspen, 1949 (Photograph, Peter Stackpole)

BELOW: Those hamburgers smelled good, but Poppa can't do the hot dogs fast enough. Pia Lindstrom looks much more patient than do I.

A New Year's Eve dance with
my favorite guy at Trail Creek Cabin,
Sun Valley, early 1950s.

A moment and a picture close to my heart—the sheriff of *High Noon* (1952) exchanges his guns for a Dixie cup and feeds his daughter some cold ice cream on the hot dusty street of Hadleyville.

ABOVE AND OPPOSITE: One of our many family rites of passage was a birthday bouquet from my parents. Lilies of the valley and sweetheart roses were perennial favorites and seemed to encapsulate my parents' sweetness, tenderness, and love.

We scrambled over the slippery rocks of the breakwater at Antibes harbor, found a perch, and spent hours sketching the little fishing boats and the nets drying over the shining black boulders. My father tended to get impatient with himself—he felt that his hand was so out of practice—but the sketches always looked pretty darn good to me. August 1959

In between shooting scenes for *The Naked Edge* in London, 1960, I made a quick sketch of "the villain."

Cooper Being Cooper

"I don't like to see exaggerated airs and exploding egos in people who are already established. No player ever rises to prominence solely on talent. They're molded by forces other than themselves. They should remember this—and at least twice a week drop to their knees and thank Providence for elevating them from cow ranches, dime-store ribbon counters and bookkeeping desks."

—Gary Cooper

How to define a person made up of so many facets and about whom millions of people have their own certain image of who and what he was? I can only jump in the middle of the lake, stir the surface with some of the details I know, and hope that the ripples will touch, inform, and add to this collective portrait of Gary Cooper.

My father was a thorough professional. He took his work seriously but not himself. He was comfortable with all kinds of people, and he could smell a phony a mile away.

Gary Cooper had strong opinions about women and beauty. In an interview for the BBC in 1957, a woman asked him, "What do you mean by womanliness?"

He answered, "A woman that is all female . . . ."

The interviewer asked, "Charm?"

Cooper said, "I find so many people that are not supposedly in the 'most beautiful' class but *are* beautiful—well, 'inside' beautiful. Something comes out only through knowing them. I suppose one of the most important things about real beauty is intelligence, and real womanliness—it's a combination of intelligence and all the instincts of womanhood, motherhood, and the beauty of girlhood. These things all sort of go in together, and they are in so many people who are not reputed beauties."

"But don't you like a bit of devil in a girl?"

He answered, "Well, that comes with it—that's very intriguing, there's no doubt of it."

The same interviewer asked him about his planned trip to the Soviet Union: "I believe you are going to Moscow now, and that you will very probably meet Mr. Khrushchev there. You've already met him in Hollywood. I believe you told him on that occasion—you congratulated him on being a very good actor."

"Yes, we met in Hollywood and we sat at this luncheon. Mr. Khrushchev talked for about an hour and forty-five minutes, and it started all very friendly until he went on and on, and finally dug up the business about not being able to go to Disneyland when it was the one thing he wanted to see—'What kind of a country is this? Are there are gangsters and something there?' Actually, it was his own security men who did not want him to go, and also it was getting late. He had talked so long that he couldn't have made Disneyland in daylight anyway! But it was very interesting and enlightening to see a man like that, the head of an important country, to analyze his emotions and his mentality at work in making a speech, just to a crowd in Hollywood."

"I can only speak for myself," my father said, "and not for other people, but for me the really satisfying things I do are offered me, free, for nothing. Ever go out in the fall and do a little hunting? See the frost on the grass and the leaves turning? Spend a day in the hills alone, or with good companions? Watch a sunset and a moonrise? Notice a bird in the wind? A stream in the woods, a storm at sea, cross the country by train, and catch a glimpse of something beautiful in the desert, or the farmlands? Free to everybody, such things as these, if you have kept your appreciation of them! *They* give you *something.*

Poppa liked to make up funny names for things. Any flying creature that resembled an insect got dubbed a "whang whang bug," such as seen here, which he drew in 1915.

In France he once completely nonplussed the maître d'hôtel in a beautiful Bordeaux restaurant by giving him a typical Cooper Western film stare and asking, "Do you have any good Bordeaux?"

Paris brought us to the Lancaster Hotel a lot in those years. I wonder whatever happened to the gentleman in the kitchen who was the recipient of my father's "lesson and humor."

My mother, father, and I had just returned from a trip to Iran in the heyday of the shah, and we landed in Paris with an enormous tin of the *best* caviar, right from the special source, His Majesty's supplier. Every evening around 6:00, we would have a private feast in our rooms: perhaps a drink, and the tin brought up from the downstairs refrigerator to be enjoyed by ourselves and any friend who happened by. Our greatest fun was to eat the caviar off the knife, with no one around to see, of course.

On this particular night, when we opened the tin there was a large quantity missing, *much* more than we had eaten the previous night. My father and mother stormed and raged about the no-good son-of-a-gun who had snitched our caviar! So with our frustration mounting, who could we accuse?

My father suddenly smiled a huge grin. "I know what we'll do," he said. He sent me out onto the terrace, where there was a long planter filled with geraniums.

Whang Whang bug

"Bring it into the living room," he said. I did. "Now, sit down, girls! We are going to finish the whole damn thing tonight." Not a tough assignment! We girls complied.

When all was gone, he told us to take some of the dirt from the planter, pack it into the caviar tin, dampen it with water, then put the top back on. It weighed just about right. Then he put the two-inch-wide red rubber band back around the top of the tin, took a pen, and very carefully marked just where the rubber band went. He rang for the waiter, who came right up. "Please, would you send this back down to the kitchen refrigerator as usual? We'll call for it tomorrow."

Poppa turned to my mother and me and laughed, and said, "I just want to see the look on the SOB's face when he goes for our caviar."

Gary Cooper and His Indian "Brothers"

My father's close friends among the Native American people are now all dead. He never told us of his own sweat lodge ceremony and his "blood-brothering." Typical of him to keep such deep and personal events to himself. But his passion for the Indian was deep. His sense of anger at the injustice done to them, deeper still. And he imbued me with a great love and respect for their culture and religion.

My father brought back arrowheads from his many treks out in the mountains or flatlands. He would put a rough, seemingly shapeless stone in my hand and begin to tell me stories about the people who had made it, chiseled and chipped away at it. Some of the stones were so ordinary they looked almost natural until he pointed out the man-made forming of the point, the remnant of the sharpened edge, the beauty of the natural granite or gouged obsidian.

ABOVE: Holding an Indian baby. (Photograph, Earl Theisen)

LEFT: On the battlefield near Little Bighorn, 1957, as photographed by Earl Theisen. Poppa revisited the battlefield of the Little Bighorn with one of the Indian elders, walking over the hill with him, treading the rocks and tall grass, examining the white markers that stick up like isolated piano ivories. He kept the thoughts and emotions of that day to himself as well.

Years later my mother and I went to see the movie *Little Big Man* with Dustin Hoffman. At the scene where we see Custer in his tent on the eve of the big assault, he is at his writing table in the candlelight signing not a peace treaty but a death warrant for the Indians encamped by the riverbanks, including innocent women and children. My mother turned to me and said in a stage whisper heard all over the balcony, "Gary always said Custer was a son of a bitch!"

Gary Cooper and Chief. (Photograph, Earl Theisen)

A 1933 portrait by my great-uncle Cedric Gibbons.

Edward Weston made this photograph of my father, then just 39.

This is a posed studio picture. Normally those look pretty remote to me, but this photo captures the mood of my father that I know so well. He would advise young actors that all they wanted to say could and should come simply through the eyes. (Photograph, A. L. Whitey Schafer, 1944)

About my father, Clifford Odets, playwright and dramatist, wrote: "He was a poet of the real. He knew all about cows, bulls, cars, and ocean tides. He had the enthusiasm of a boy. He could always tell you his first vivid impression of a thing. He had an old-fashioned politeness, but he said nothing casually."

OPPOSITE: Is this an actor, a fisherman, or an elegant tightrope walker balancing with a fishing pole? Bob Capa, the great war correspondent/photographer, captured a moment in Sun Valley of sheer Cooper elegance and grace, every sinew of his body placed just right. The creek would not catch him this day.

Big festivities in simple little Brentwood, 1949. The streets were closed to traffic and Poppa was made honorary mayor. Proclamation in hand, he rides off into the night.

Poppa loved to sleep. He could do it anywhere, anytime.
The surface was immaterial. Bingo was the mascot in
Aspen of those simpler days in the late forties. He knew
everyone and everyone knew him. His owners, Ellie and
Fred Islin, let him have complete roaming privileges, but
often on a cold but sun-warmed day you'd find him
snoozing in front of the Jerome Hotel on Main Street or
the adjoining epicure Tea Shoppe. Here, dreaming of
catching the perfect rabbit, he is joined by a friend,
dreaming perhaps of the perfect run down the mountain.

1-2-3 . . . and he's *out!* Richard Widmark recalls a scene he and Coop were shooting on location for *Garden of Evil.* The two actors had taken their positions on the ground around a campfire, stretched out, using their saddles for pillows. They had rehearsed the dialogue several times and were waiting. Henry Hathaway, the director, finally yelled, "Roll 'em!"

Dick spoke his lines addressed to my father, and there was silence.

"Cut! Take two!" came the voice behind the camera. Again, silence, and then a snore. Poppa was sleeping soundly, oblivious to the chaos, cameras, and crew around him.

"What the hell!" Henry stormed over to the two cowboys.

Richard was suppressing a chuckle. He shouted, "Gary, you're on!"

Poppa opened his eyes and went right into the dialogue, never missing a beat. So much for pre-performance jitters! However, maybe that was his way of handling it. He never said.

In the South Pacific

The actor Gary Cooper felt embarrassed when his 1943-44 USO tour of the American bases in the South Pacific took him to a makeshift wooden stage set up in the jungle, and he had to appear with entertainers like Bob Hope, Jack Benny, Una Merkel, Dorothy Lamour. In an interview, his own words capture the spirit of that time:

"One night we hit a small cloudburst. I thought the show would be called off, and was dozing in my tent when an officer came in to say that 15,000 kids were sitting in the rain on a muddy slope waiting for us. We went out.

"Canvas tarps had been hung over the stage. A few lads stood by with poles, and whenever a tarp sagged with collected rainwater, one of them would give the bulge a poke. No telling whether the water would be dumped offstage or on. We went through our act once and were starting over when some kid hollered, 'Hey, Coop, how about Lou Gehrig's farewell speech to the Yankees?' His suggestion caught on. The picture had just played there, and the boys began to chant in unison for the farewell speech.

"'Give me a minute to get it straight,' I said into the microphone. 'I don't want to leave out anything.' I sat down to one side to write out the words. The rain was thundering down on the tarps, and every now and then a pole would slip and I would get a gallon of water down my neck, but I finally got the speech written down as I remembered it. It was a silent bunch that listened to the lines:

I've been walking on ballfields for sixteen years, and I've never received anything but kindness and encouragement from you fans. I've had the great honor to have played with these great veteran ballplayers on my left—Murderer's Row—our championship team of 1927. I've had the further honor of living with and playing with these men on my right—the Bronx Bombers, the Yankees of today. I've been given fame and undeserved praise by the boys up there behind the wire in the press box—my friends—the sportswriters. I've worked under the two greatest managers of all time—Miller Huggins and Joe McCarthy.

I have a mother and father who fought to give me health and a solid background in my youth. I have a wife—a companion for life—who has shown me more courage than I ever knew.

People all say that I've had a bad break. But—today—I consider myself the luckiest man on the face of the earth.

"That was all. They were the words of a brave American who had only a short time to live, and they meant something to those kids in the Pacific. After that, no matter where we went—Dobodura, Myline Bay, Goodenough Island, Hollandia, Lae, Darwin, and a score of other places on our 24,000-mile island-hopping tour, we got requests for the speech."

Who looks happier—the boys on being with my father, or he being with them?
I can't imagine how awed my father must have felt facing this "sea" of admiring army folk.

Poppa loved having conversations with guys. He was interested in their lives, their work, and here—wouldn't he just have loved driving that engine? (Photograph, Peter Stackpole, 1957)

OPPOSITE: In this picture, the approaching train, white smoke and all, looks like the *High Noon* train coming into town. In fact, it's coming into the little station in Aspen. We had just placed a quarter on the tracks and were repeating another little family "fun" ritual that took place whenever we were around train tracks and a train was coming. First a quarter or a penny would go on the railroad track. Next we would lie on our stomachs, ear to the steel rail, and listen for the coming of the train. We would then step back and watch for the tons of steel to pass us, followed by a gleeful search for the flattened coin. It was so paper thin and smooth, it always delighted and amazed me. (Photograph, Peter Stackpole, 1950)

The grand opening of a new Hilton hotel in Madrid brought a
planeload of guests from the U.S. and Europe for gala festivities. One
afternoon's entertainment took us to a beautiful ranch mostly devoted to
the breeding of bulls for the bullfight. The owners invited my father
to be part of the demonstration to see if the young heifers had the
makings of "brave bulls." My father felt brave himself with that critter
charging him until his eyeglasses fell off. With blurred vision and a
two-hundred-and-fifty-pound heifer heading straight for his stomach,
he dropped the cape and ran like hell to a safe place behind
the barrier. (Photograph, Yale Joel, 1953)

Back to the Homestead

My father wanted to revisit some of the places of his youth, and in 1957 he set out with his buddy Earl Theisen, who also was one of the top photographers of his day. This "returning to the old homestead" adventure took them to such towns as Jackson, West Yellowstone (where Poppa had driven a tourist bus in his early days), Hardin, Billings, Bozeman, Helena (his birthplace), Glacier, Logan Pass, Ronan, Missoula, Philipsburg, Butte. Some of the following candid photos capture genuine moments of his sentimental trip.

In a saloon somewhere between Yellowstone and Butte.

Sighting gun on railroad tracks—a typical Cooper position.

Poppa fishing? Thinking? Both? He could sit in silence for hours. If it was traveling in a car with someone, I gather he would drive them crazy, because he just wouldn't talk if he didn't want to—"Thinkin'," he would say. That was that! But if the guys and the circumstances were right, he and they could have a real gabfest.

When he was in Africa, my father had just been swimming and thought nothing of the water in his ears, until a loud gun blast was fired quite close to him. The reverberation of the liquid in his left ear damaged his eardrum, and thereafter he had very little hearing on that side. So if he didn't want to talk while in a car with someone he would ask them to drive, take the passenger seat, open the right window, and with his "good ear" to the wind, he couldn't hear a darn thing.

A Cooper moment. His words were probably something like "Hot ziggety!" or "By damn!"

Doggies make mistakes, even house-broken ones. Little "Bali Beans," our Maltese, had a bad habit, and when caught in the act everyone got thrown outside in the garden to "think it over." Now they want back in, but Poppa, the stern disciplinarian, bends over and has a long heart-to-heart through the glass sliding door. Iris, the innocent, looks on. (Photograph, Willie Rizzo, 1959)

Family Time

Gary Cooper's roots go back to Houghton Regis in Bedfordshire, England. His father was born there in 1865. The family owned several farms, and had a dairy business in London. Many generations of Coopers had been farmers, but by the mid-nineteenth century the tales of the American West intrigued some of the family, in particular Walter Cooper, my father's uncle. He saved money and made the trip to Montana—and then encouraged my grandfather, Charles, age seventeen, to strike out himself and work his way across the ocean. Mixing a couple of paying jobs in Montana, and studying Shakespeare (a passion of his), Charles then went to law school and ultimately became a lawyer and a judge.

My grandmother Alice Brazier Cooper's family was originally French, from near Lyons. My grandmother was born in Gillingham, in Kent, England. She made her way to Montana to visit her brother in 1891. She met Charles Cooper in Helena when he helped her with some financial matters. They fell in love and married in 1894. She had very strong, clear blue eyes, and beautiful hands, which she used emphatically while talking. My father, with his actor's eye for economy of movement, used to lovingly suggest, "Mother, stop windmilling your hands!"

Alice was a resourceful and creative woman. Aside from raising the family and running the ranch, she was also a female photographer, and one who did her own developing, rare in those days. They were a close family, with solid values. The judge's decisions tended to be on the side of the underdog against the system, and conversations around the family dinner table must have reflected a basic philosophy of fairness and concern for human rights. In time, Alice's desire for the boys to be more civilized led her to convince their father that some time at a proper English school would be useful. So off my father and his brother Arthur went, to Dunstable, for about three years.

When my father returned home to Helena, he had his heart set on becoming a commercial artist. Rather than pursue his academic studies, he was much more interested in sketching and daydreaming than in studying. In later years, though, he loved reading history and I think tried to make up for the "lost" books, especially those about the old West.

Having a "hero" or mythic-image kind of man as my father colored life in extraordinary ways for us as a family. Life was a very large, vivid canvas on which real people lived and struggled and overcame.

The Three Coopers

We were often spoken of as "The Coopers" by our friends in Hollywood. Ours was a unique family togetherness that was obvious and operative. So many of the daily-life things we did were just like any other family's activities. But for us there was a plethora of extraordinary situations as well. Meeting with the pope, being introduced to the royal family in England, a wild late-night ride in Paris with the shah of Iran—it was as glamorous as it sounds even today, but always tempered by the down-to-earth values of my parents.

We had a number of family traditions, one of them being a Sunday morning swim in the ocean after Mass. My mother and I would wear our bathing suits under our clothes, then after church we'd zip up the street to our house in Brentwood, get Poppa, who had been studying or working in his gun room or catching

Biarritz, in the mid-1950s. Oceans, seas, beaches—a
place where we always connected one-to-one as a family.
We studied how birds would ride the air currents, the
thermals, circling higher without a wingbeat. "Look!
Look at the beauty of that!" my father would say.
"LOOK!"

forty more winks, pile the dogs in the car, and take off for Santa Monica. We'd look for an empty piece of beach and hit the ground running. Often it was cold—if not the air, then the water temperature, and we'd run, walk, talk, throw big sticks for Arno, our boxer. Sometimes we'd bring six-foot-long pillowcases, zippers at one end. What fun to run on the sand until they were filled with air, then make for the breaking waves and pounce on top of our airbag pillows and ride the waves into shore. They made for very fast, snorty bodysurfing and the dogs would go crazy.

Come "go home time," we'd change under our terry robes, trudge to the car, and head home to warm up and to another "ritual"—starting up the barbecue, where we'd do special hot dogs, polishing away three, four, or five dogs each.

The surround of those hours was such a sense of well-being. Our family was purring in enjoyment and savoring it all—the salt water still tingling our bodies, the mix of fragances from the nearby eucalyptus, the orange blossoms or jasmine, the cut grass.

Another standout memory—my father's delight in smelling flowers, especially roses. One day in Grasse, in the south of France, he got his fill. The entire town had turned out for the annual rose fete. That year, 1956, my father was part of the festivities. We were put on a small float that glided through this sea of flowers. All around us people were madly throwing millions of rose petals—it was literally raining flowers on everyone, a ticker-tape parade of living bits of nature.

Crowd scenes like that usually scared me a bit, but this was different. The adulation for "Coop" swooped us up in the excitement and celebration of the event itself. That day was everything.

The late 1940s were times of change for the Cooper family. The "perfect" family image crashed, as all human and certainly Hollywood "perfection"

crashes. I know my father had a great reputation as a ladies' man. I never found that surprising, and understood the temptations that being an actor offered, as well as his being a damn good-looking man who appealed to every female, young or old.

None of this impacted my life until 1946, when he made *The Fountainhead* and fell in love with his leading lady, Patricia Neal. Their relationship disrupted the family's stability, and we went through some tough times. Eventually my father moved out. Although my parents separated for several years, somehow during all that time they maintained for me a sense of unity. There was never a pitting of one against the other, nor arguing within my earshot.

Yet children sense family troubles and tensions. So it was something of a relief when one afternoon at the Hotel Jerome in Aspen my mother told me that my father thought he was in love with another woman. We embraced each other and then she told me to go into the other room, where my father was standing. He was looking out a window, obviously very upset. "Go give him a hug," she said. "He's very upset and you must know all this has absolutely *nothing* to do with you, nor does it change our love for you, and how the three of us are."

They both handled that moment as well as it could be done. I was ten years old and grew up very quickly that day. What I remember about that period was my mother's strength, composure, and beauty, and my father's ulcers. He was not going through this whole thing lightly, and it took a toll on his health.

A publicly exposed rocky marriage became a way of life that we shared with a lot of other families out there, so that *too* became sort of normal.

While he enjoyed his bachelor life, my father realized this was not really making him happy. Eventually he decided, as he said, "to take a long walk alone." But the walk was not overnight. Three years or so passed, in which the Cooper family startled everyone by our unorthodox togetherness. In the middle of separate lives, we would occasionally spend some time together, vacationing and happily doing family things whenever possible. No matter what the press was saying, or who was going out with whom, I could always see the love between my parents. This gave me great stability and comfort.

My mother was a terribly shy person, someone who had never been aware of her own beauty and had hidden behind a facade of self-confidence. Those years gave her the opportunity to find her own self in ways she had not known before. She went out a lot, developed a fantastic reputation as a hostess, and I think impressed my father with her own glamour, spunk, and verve. She combined all the elements that were important to him in a woman. She was smart, understood men, and was never vindictive or bitter. Eventually life brought their two paths together again.

In the early 1950s, my father made a couple of pictures back-to-back that kept him away from the United States. The following letters to my mother and me reach out from Apia, Western Samoa, where he was shooting a picture called *Return to Paradise*. The actors had been in place for weeks, but no equipment had arrived:

July 24, 1952
Because we crossed the international dateline twice, left Fiji Monday morning and arrived in Samoa the preceding Sunday. And we have been sitting here without stuff to make a picture, and no word from the ship yet. (She's supposed to radio when she's a thousand miles from our island, but no word has come as yet.) . . . I'm already resigned to letting the days come and go without stirring up my ulcer further.

I miss my dear girls. You seem so far away and it seems so long ago that I saw you both standing in the afternoon sun of Chez Shields and waving good-bye

to me. That's the sweetest picture I'll ever see.

Well, you just barely set foot on this ground here, and you know why Gauguin stayed. It's more beautiful than you imagine. The villages are like parks. The fales (houses) are all light palm-thatched roofs, open on all sides. They decorate everything with flowers, and the shoreline is nearly one solid continuation of villages. And the people dress and look exactly as Gauguin painted the Tahitians years ago.

Big disappointment—the swimming!!! Raw sewage goes into the water. There are places, however, where the water is clear, and I am trying to locate them. I hear the sharks, barracuda and eels are plentiful. . . .

I miss you both so much. Gosh, you really feel half a million miles removed from anywhere. Love, your Poppa

And a follow-up letter from him eight days later:

August 1, 1952
Dear Girls,
The ship came over the horizon Monday. No word from them on account of the different wavelength, and about a mile beyond the reef we identified her as not a local craft. Everyone's spirits rose, big excitement and much work unloading a hundred and twenty tons of equipment. The picture is really going to start, and now we have been hard at it for two days. We leave here at seven o'clock, and return here at seven-thirty or eight in the evening, and are plenty pooped. This is just a hurried note to tell you I miss you and I'm feeling fine. The mail closes soon, so I shall get this done quickly. After tomorrow, no mail in or out for another ten days. A plane that stops here comes in on a ten-day loop from New Zealand to Fiji, to Samoa, to Ruratouva and back to New Zealand. In the meantime, you wonder what's going on in the world and how many zillions of miles away it is.

In September 1937, the Coopers' life expanded—I came along. After an ocean swim guided through the waves by my father and Joel McCrea, my mother had dinner and then there was a mad dash for the hospital. My mother's old chaperone, Elvira—Vivi—took the nurse reins and helped care for me as she had cared for my mother as a little child.

Mine were the usual protective parents, probably a bit more so in the light of Hollywood notoriety and the recent Lindbergh baby kidnapping. My nursery windows on the ground floor had iron frames for extra protection, and there was a guard who patrolled the grounds at night. We had lots of outdoor room, however, in the beautiful gardens, and there were animals galore. For me, it was utopia.

Poppa getting my pitching arm ready. My parents were always letting me see things from the heights, in this case from Baldy Mountain. "The view from the top," that was a metaphor for our life, I guess—how far you can see, how limitless is the horizon. (Photograph, Robert Capa)

A budding Olympic racer. Or a hopeful one.

A family musical complete with a canine choir. I
was determined to learn to play the accordion. Poppa
noodled around with his harmonica a lot and my mother,
fresh from Hawaii, tried her hand at the ukelele.
Our impromptu concert certainly excited the dogs, Arno
and Gretel, who joined in at every opportunity. Was
it to drown us out?

One day we were sitting around the pool. My mother was wearing a hat she had decorated, influenced by a Hawaiian vacation. We started hamming it up, and soon somebody noticed that the pose was less than original. Hanging in our library was Renoir's *Young Girl in a Hat*—some coincidence!

After work or on weekends, the three of us would cycle way up in the hills above our Brentwood house, passing the homes of our friends Frank Capra, William Wellman, Tyrone and Annabella Power, Watson Webb, Laurence Olivier, Van and Evie Johnson, and Cesar Romero.

OPPOSITE: The Addams family had nothing on us! We explored this so-called haunted house—actually a burnt-out relic of Aspen's Victorian days—and heard, maybe, some ghosts moving across the creaking floors. Here we are looking our most ghoulish for Pete Stackpole of *Life* magazine, 1949.

A family night on the town. My grandmother Alice loved restaurants, cameras, the fun of being Gary Cooper's mother. And was she strong willed! At one point in my father's boyhood she stood on the porch of their ranch house and with a shotgun held off an escaped group of prisoners from a chain gang until the guards ran up the riverbank and recaptured them.

The Traveling Coopers

Airport arrivals with Poppa in Europe, such as this circa 1950, were usually greeted with bunches of flowers, lots of press, cameras, and much hullabaloo, which he took in his good-natured stride.

My parents and grandmother
Veronica Shields were seated in a
huge amphitheater in a German for-
est near the Hungarian border in
1956. This evening, which was to
have been a benefit to raise money
for Hungarian refugees who had
been fleeing the Soviets and coming
into Germany, turned into a prayer
service. It seems that afternoon
there had been a massive Russian
troop movement, and the one escape
route was sealed off. Instead of cele-
brating with us, the special section
reserved for the Hungarians was
empty and in utter blackness. We lit
candles, and the whole space flick-
ered and glowed as we prayed for
the survival of the Hungarians.

OPPOSITE: The excitement of the approaching audience with the pope touched all of us. Those were the days when the dress code for meeting the pope was black, long sleeves, and veil. This was way before Vatican II, and now it seems strange to me that for a supposedly joyous occasion one had to dress as if at a funeral. Anyway, it added to the drama, and we lined up in an ornate gilded room in the Vatican with about twenty other VIP guests. My father was years away from becoming a Catholic, but the pomp and ritual were awesome, and everyone was highly nervous. We had bought rosaries and medals to be blessed by His Holiness, and Poppa had a fair share in his hands and over his wrists. The great doors swung open and a Swiss Guard thumped ceremoniously on the floor with an intricately carved gilt staff to announce the pope's arrival. Then His Eminence flowed in through the door—slim, white-robed, pale—and started down the line of guests. Just as he was nearly in front of my father, we all genuflected, but with his stiff back, Poppa lost his balance a bit and in that moment dropped all his beads, medals, and cards. They went rolling and scattering all over the floor, under the pontiff's robes, the carpet, and into other people's shoes. And there was the American actor Gary Cooper groping around in monumental embarrassment, trying to scoop up the mementos with Pius XII looking down and patiently smiling.

RIGHT: Being presented to Her Majesty, Queen Elizabeth, London, 1953.

Three American
tourists captured by the
ancient beauty of the
Parthenon. My father's
strong feeling for art and
history made this visit
especially moving.

Cooper guzzling ancient wine from a long-buried amphora off the Antibes coastline, mid-1950s. Our friends from Greece, Basil and Elise Goulandris, are sitting in the prow of a slightly smaller "ship" than they are used to!

Exploring underground caves, France, 1956. We all gasped at the awesome sight of stalagmites and stalactites forming, still growing, hundreds of feet underground—their "drip, drip, drip" forming for millions of years. We started collecting mineral specimens, quartz crystals, and rocks that glowed with unreal colors when you put them under black light.

Weekend strolls often led us to the Seine and the sidewalk markets. When my father was on location in Paris filming *Love in the Afternoon,* he wrote me this enthusiastic letter describing his activities:

Gay?? Paris—Saturday evening
Hello angel cakes:

Just got through with a shouting session over the phone with Prinzmetal and it looks like he'll have to come over here in order to conclude any business deal, the connection was so terrible.

I'm so sorry I missed talking to you last Sunday. Mama and I had a good connection. You can't imagine how mad I am that I can't see what's going on with the new house but I know it's in very capable hands, yours and mama's and Jones's. I was very thrilled with the snapshots Mama sent—also your painting!

Of the Biarritz crowd Ned and Molly are still here, W. Donohue, the De Bendens, Dolly O'Brian. Liz, Tex, and Lex just left for Holland. Darryl Zanuck, Akim Tamiroff, etc. etc. no chance to talk French. But I'm playing golf and slowly getting the turning muscles back in shape.

I wrote Mama I'd tell you about the opera. Remember the big spooky looking Paris opera building? Well, I went to see a ballet with singing. It was magnificently staged, the costumes were very colorful and interesting from an artistic standpoint, but most interesting was the place itself. It's very old and reeks of tradition and is very weird architecturally. One series of stairways goes seven stories underground to what was an underground river. The stage is enormous and goes thirteen stories above the floor level of the stage—shucks! I can't

describe it! I'll mail you the book they gave me on it and it would be good to keep. As I told Mama, the ballet girls were limbering up between acts at the same rail and mirrors that Degas painted, the costumes, the smells eg: when the rose ballet goes on the original air conditioning system blows rose scent all through the theatre. And when the volcano erupts (in the show) you smell incense and brimstone!! Well, it's a must for our next trip to Paris. Real atmosphere, whew!

I wish you would give grandmother a call Oct. 10th because it's her birthday and it would make her feel awfully good to wish her happy birthday. She'll be eighty years old.

I'll sign off for now and will write you tout suite? I love you my angel and give Mama puss a big smack for me. XXXXXXX Poppa

One of the Paris activities my father enjoyed was going along with "his girls" to a couture fashion show. Always a man of contrasts, he loved seeing my mother in shooting jackets, jeans, shorts—or in an elegant, beautifully designed suit or dress created by a top artist of fashion. At home in Hollywood, she got many clothes from Irene (one of MGM's top designers, and her aunt by marriage). When in New York, she and her mother were friends of a young and very talented designer named Bill Blass. But when they hit Paris, my father loved to come along for the shopping. He especially admired the artistry, talent, and natural elegance of the great designer Hubert de Givenchy, who became a cherished friend. Neither of these men, in the light of their enormous fame, ever lost their innate simplicity and natural warmth.

"See Naples and Die"

One day in the paper my mother discovered a new organization called the Foster Parents Plan for War Children. She and my father immediately signed up. We exchanged letters and financially supported the education and basic necessities of a poverty- and war-devastated family. Raffaela Gravina—the child's furrowed face looked out from the photograph she sent us—was my first personal connection with the harsh lives of those who share this planet.

One day, something out of a Hollywood story fell into place. It was summertime, Poppa had some personal appearance tours to do, and we were going to Italy. So the three of us planned to visit Raffaela and what was left of her family.

We got to Naples, piled into two cars, and headed off toward the mountains. The little town of Mignano di Monte Lungo was ten miles south of Monte Cassino. Its poverty level before the war had been severe, and now, after the bombing, it was totally devastated. The driver suddenly stopped the car. As the dust settled, I couldn't believe what was around us. We were about a city block's length from the actual edge of the wooden shacks and earthen and stone houses that were the beginning of the town. Broad streaks of white paint in the dirt road spelled out the town's welcome: "VIVA GARY COOPER, VIVA GARY COOPER."

Above our heads, strung between two scrawny trees, was stretched a banner with "WELCOME GARY" waving and flapping hard in the hot wind. Below it, and as far as we could see, the street was solid people calling out, smiling, crying, handkerchiefs fluttering and colored streamers blowing. It was as if we were a liberation squad freeing them from obscurity and neglect.

I was overwhelmed with all the excitement and affection that my father's visit was causing. I had seen the poverty of Mexico, and been sobered by it, but this had come out of war. This innocent little town had been all but blasted away during the war, and suddenly we had a personal identification with it. There we saw the little girl from the letters and photos, surrounded by her mother and brothers.

They crowded around us, and I saw such a look of compassion on my father's face it made me want to cry; but there was no time for that. Interpreters were working overtime, photographers too. So much energy, not enough words, or the right ones, for a moment like this.

Momma was incredible. She had a great knack for putting anybody at ease, in any situation, and she did it here. She chatted along with Raffaela and her mother, and before long it was time for lunch.

Another shock. The streets were filled with tables end-to-end, some covered in red checked cloth, some in old oilcloth, or a few once-lovely pieces of linen. It seemed like there was a table from every home in town. And then, the most moving of all—the food laid out there must have been the rations of every family in town for two weeks.

We sat down to platters of antipasto, sausage, pizza, spaghetti, sauces, garlic-soaked breads, more sausages—the feast so lovingly prepared for this star from the fantasy world of every woman's romantic dream and every man's heroic self. The whole town watched us carefully and observed each chew, each swallow. What they hadn't realized was that after so many hours in the heat the food had become rancid. Poor Poppa, he couldn't get away with saying "No, thank you" to anyone. Each person offering the plate looked crushed, wounded, if he even started to say No. Finally, by five o'clock we had begun to move out. Good-byes were wet with happy tears, promises to continue, of course, our correspondence and help. Slowly we drove away.

Poppa paid a high price for eating so much. We made the train in Naples, but he was feeling sicker and sicker, and by the time we got to the Rome station he was white-green. It was a good five days later that he emerged from the hotel, many pounds lighter. "See Naples and die" became a standing family expression for years after.

And what did Poppa say about that day? In typical Cooper fashion, he carried his deepest-running thoughts and emotions silently and didn't say much. But his face and his arms around Raffaela, and his smile with the people of the town up there on the side of the mountain, told me more than words.

My parents and I with Raffaela and her mother.

Poppa loved teaching, and Peter, the Corgi, knows just how to get all the words of praise he wants from his professor. My mother and I used our time in front of the TV to make needlepoint pillows of reproductions of works of art that we loved. We had finished two Gauguins (on the couch) and each of us here is working on a van Gogh. (Photograph, Willie Rizzo)

Living Our Good Life

More than any words say, a moment in time captured by Slim Aarons as New Year's chimes ring in—mother, daughter, husband, father. It reminds me of these lines from a Francis Thompson poem, *New Year's Chimes:* "This is the song the stars sing /And a million songs are as song of one."

A Drink to Die For—

About twice a month, Poppa's mother, Alice, would come for barbecue and Bloody Marys, the family drink then. She still had an appetite equal to her days back on the family ranch in Montana, when she would swing an axe at 20 degrees below zero to break open bales of hay. Now, at 84, age and digestive problems didn't slow her down at all.

Poppa liked to tease her, so one day he took a rather large syringe, a joke kit phony needle and plunger, filled it with tomato juice and walked over to her. "Mother," he said, "I'm gonna make you a really good Bloody Mary today," as he held the false needle up to his arm's vein. He made a withdrawing motion and good rich red filled the syringe.

"*Son!*" Grandmother exclaimed, eyes wide in horror. "What *are* you doing?"

Around this time, one of our new family members, a dachshund named Dyna, also showed a predeliction for Bloody Marys. Dyna's delight was to lap up any spilled Bloody Mary and then make for a cozy spot in my father's lap to sleep it off.

In our new house in Holmby Hills, designed by architect Quincy Jones, my father and I shared a work space. One wall opened up to reveal his gun collection, workbench, and tools. My painter's easel often was the drying-off place for our diving suits, regulators, and other scuba equipment. By this time, around 1959, Poppa left the painting pretty much to me. I felt he always had an itching to get back to it. But there was never enough time. (Photograph, Willie Rizzo)

Family and Friends

The Coopers were totally comfortable with anybody, any place, simple or grand. Diversity was probably the key word. There was only one main requirement—no phonies allowed!

Hemingway used to criticize my mother for using the term *good friend*—"Ah! A person is either a friend, or not a friend!" The word "good" was superfluous—"friend" said it all.

Two men: one who would become president and one who was an actor. Each, in his own way, became an icon of the American hero throughout the world. Both had lives that were to end tragically too young. This photo was taken in the early 1940s.

Pat deCicco, Rocky, and Chuck Heston, 1958. Pat and Gary were big buddies, though not always with my mother's approval: "Guys will be guys," bonding stuff! Pat was very funny. He loved pheasant and duck hunting, travel, and women. Much married, he moved in many fast lanes, European and Latin American. He was an old friend of Howard Hughes, and to Pat's credit, never told any of the stories that would have caused the equivalent of today's feeding frenzy in the tabloids. He took all his confidences to the grave.

My father especially enjoyed working with Chuck Heston and liked him a lot, as a colleague and as a friend. Doing their own underwater fights and stunts filming *The Wreck of the Mary Deare* was pretty tough work for both guys.

In 1953, Gary Cooper and Tony Quinn were working together in Mexico making a film called *Blowing Wild*. In this picture, the two fellows have just been told they won Academy Awards—my father for Best Actor in *High Noon* and Tony for Best Supporting Actor in *Viva Zapata!*

Tennis was a big part of the California lifestyle, and the
Pacific Southwest championships in 1935 drew lots of fans,
including, from left to right, my father, tennis champion/
budding actor Francis X. Shields (Brooke Shields's grandfather), Cedric Gibbons, the Mexican actress Delores Del
Rio (Mrs. Gibbons), and my mother, Cedric's niece.

One of our early United States tennis heroes and champions, Sydney Wood, is floating down the Hudson River with the Coopers, circa 1930s. Sydney always said Rocky had the best forehand of any nonprofessional he'd ever played with.

En route to one of our weekend excursions. This one, across the border in Tijuana for a bullfight in the mid-1950s, included the literary agent Swifty Lazar and Lauren Bacall.

On one of these occasions, Rocky, who normally could not stand the sight of blood *anywhere,* and who would shut her eyes during the major part of the bullfight, came equipped with a movie camera, as their friend Carlos Aruzza was fighting that day. To steel herself for what was to come, she downed several tequilas at lunch, and sailed through the afternoon fortified and numbed to all the gore—filming all the time. Two weeks later, at the Beverly Hills camera shop, editing the developed footage, Momma and I sat in the projection room. Images of the bullfight splashed on the screen, in all its pageantry and color, drama and daring. But suddenly, next to me, the stalwart photographer Rocky, at the sight of all the blood, had fainted dead away.

The golfing great Ben Hogan, visiting on the set of *Task Force* in 1949, tries to get my father to relax and change his grip. "Dr. Hogan" is trying to help Coop correct a consistent tendency to "hook the damn ball."

Our whole family was close to Ben and Valerie, his wife. My grandfather Paul Shields and Ben were truly buddies, and my good fortune as a young golfer was to walk around many miles of golf course with Hogan and our family. Watching the best is truly inspirational, and I had several impromptu lessons from the master himself.

Henry Ford stopping to visit on the set of *The Naked Edge* in London, 1960. My father's costar, Deborah Kerr, and Ann Ford are probably listening once again to some car talk. Henry and Ann Ford, close dear friends—part of another facet of Gary Cooper's life. You couldn't pry Henry and my father apart when they were off in a corner discussing cars or their cantankerous golf game.

This was the era of famous nightclubs—El Morocco, the Stork Club, the Copacabana—when elegance of dress and behavior was the code. Here, left to right, are Marius Ericson, a member of the F.I.S. ski team and brother of Stein Ericson, the great skier and team leader, Rocky, and close friends Virgil and Betty Sherrill on either side of Gary. My father enjoyed the nightlife under the white palm trees of El Morocco—for a bit! Then he was always eager to head out, back under real pine trees and the stars.

OPPOSITE: My father, the great director Fred Zinnemann, and Grace Kelly discussing some upcoming scenes in *High Noon*. (Photograph, Schuyler Crail)

Fred Zinnemann—A Special Friendship

Fred Zinnemann—no introduction needed! A few of his credits as director include *From Here to Eternity, The Men, Oklahoma!, The Nun's Story, The Day of the Jackal, A Man for All Seasons,* and, of course, with my father, *High Noon.*

Fred's greatness as an artist was surpassed only by his depth as a friend. Fred wanted to give Rene, his wife of twenty-six years, a special wedding gift. Knowing how much this would mean to her, he asked my parents to help arrange for them to be remarried in a Catholic ceremony, with my father as best man. So it happened that the last time Poppa ever left the house in 1961 was to stand up with Fred at the wedding service, held at Good Shepherd Church (or, "Our Lady of the Cadillacs," as Roz Russell dubbed it); four weeks later he was buried from that same altar. In spite of great pain, Poppa wanted to be there for Fred. After the ceremony, we came home to toast life and celebrate love.

Our friendship with Fred Zinnemann was unique and deep. It was eleven years from the time he and Poppa first worked together to the end of my father's life. They were both quiet men who seemed to communicate on another level.

In the moments just after my father died, I was in my mother's bedroom and picked up a ringing telephone. I don't know why I did that *then,* as other people were taking all the phone calls, but it was Fred, calling from the south of France to give us all his love. Since then, we've often spoken of his uncanny timing and concluded that at some level Fred *knew* my father had just died and was embracing the three of us.

Ernest Hemingway and Gary Cooper—Papa and Poppa

Tillie Arnold recalls that it was Gene Van Gelder who arranged for Coop and Hemingway to meet one another in Sun Valley. This was the first photo of the two guys, taken in 1940, at the start of being lifelong comrades.

In these early days, things seemed simple and unspoiled. The Hemingways and the Coopers stayed in rooms at The Lodge. The Ram restaurant, where everyone gathered, was open for lunch and dinner. As Ernest said, "I never had it so good in the West."

It was amusing to see them together. Cooper always looked impeccable, even though totally casual. Ernest could have cared less. Ernest had a way of making fun things even more fun, and everyone looked to him to lead the pack. Although the guys liked having a good stiff drink, it was *never* part of their "fun" to drink and handle guns. And if they were out hunting with women along, in true chivalrous fashion, Ernest would always place them so they would get the best shots.

The Coopers loved Sun Valley and it became their getaway place, satisfying my father's need for mountains and wild country and my mother's love of sports year-round.

When Ernest Hemingway became part of the life of the valley, the two men met and formed a bond, perhaps unlikely, that existed whether in Idaho or Cuba or Paris or New York for as long as they lived.

Gary Cooper, Ernest Hemingway, Rocky Cooper.
(Photograph, Lloyd Arnold, 1940)

Rocky earned her medals as California State Women's
Skeet Champion. Here, gun hot, my parents and Ernest
are at the skeet field watching the trajectory of the
skeet pigeons, checking the valley winds. Rocky shot
with the guys and often beat them. My father loved it!
(Photograph, Robert Capa, 1940)

"They went thataway" could refer to the bad guys in a Gary Cooper Western, or, here, with Ernest Hemingway telling "Beartracks" (Taylor Williams) and Coop where the next batch of ducks were likely to fly in from. (Photograph, Robert Capa)

The adventures with Ernest would fill chapters. My father wrote about one of them:

"I can't leave Sun Valley without mention of a safari we had up there, conducted by Ernest Hemingway. The party included Hemingway, Martha Gellhorn, Bob Taylor, Barbara Stanwyck, Rocky, and me. Pheasant was our objective, and Hemingway so impressed Bob and me with his knowledge of pheasant hunting that we didn't have a word to say. He deployed us like a general directing maneuvers, Bob and Barbara down the slope about a quarter-mile to a patch of likely-looking cover, Rocky and me to a blackberry patch straight across the field.

"'And Martha and I will take the upper corner,' Hemingway said. 'I know this field, and it's real good. Don't shoot if you flush a bird or two. In fact, don't shoot until you hear me holler. Is that clear?'

"We started out. Bob and Barbara got to their patch of brush just as Rocky and I reached ours. As I looked at Bob to see how he was coming, the air around him exploded with birds. If he hadn't been holding his gun, he could have caught a dozen in his bare hands. Rocky made a move, and there was another explosion of pheasant all around us. They nearly blew my hat off. I held my gun poised, waiting for Hemingway. He knew his pheasant, all right. Far beyond Bob's or my range, the two flocks joined and swung right over his head.

"'Fire!' he yelled, and let go with both barrels. It took a minute for the air to clear of feathers. I looked down at Bob, and he looked back at me. The Nebraska boy and the Montana boy, raised in pheasant country, had been took. At that moment, a lone bird went by, and Bob brought him down.

"Barbara and Rocky looked at the dead bird and gulped. 'I think I'll stick to clay pigeons,' announced Rocky.

"'I hate hunting!' wailed Barbara."

Whatever they were talking about here, it surely was not about work—both men, Poppa and
Papa, *never* did. (Photograph, Robert Capa, 1940)

Sometimes they would mosey around the little town of Ketchum, checking out the local stores.
One day after a varied shopping spree, they hit the bookstore and picked up some interesting
reading material. In one of the books bought that day, Ernest wrote,
To the Coopers,
To make something to supplement the Idaho statesman as reading matter.
With good luck always,
Ernest Hemingway
On the day we got books, October 5, 1940

The book was a copy of *For Whom the Bell Tolls.*

A road stretches straight to the horizon. A good day of hunting is over. Satisfaction. For the guys and Martha Gellhorn, Hemingway's wife, it was a long quiet trek back to the cars. They didn't need chatter to prove friendship. (Photograph, Robert Capa, 1940)

Play Time

What elements hold family life together? One of them, I believe, is a sense of play. For me, play was a way of learning about all of life—people, relationships, character, sportsmanship, and, strange as it may seem, even prayer. My mother was the family choreographer—being taken by a new idea she might have heard of, or new people met in an unusual field, usually meant that by the next day she would have exposed us to it. She orchestrated and filled our days with a variety of activities, and my father loved to be organized by her.

She worked at being entertaining to my father, and provided interesting diversions for him. He was always game to try new sports. Even if he didn't do all of it himself, he got a real charge out of seeing "his girls" perform, or struggle, as the case might have been.

He equally enjoyed being alone, totally absorbed for hours, in his gun room, building model airplanes and boats, fitting arrows with feathers for better trajectory. Just as good was being outside working on his cars, or in the orchard breaking up the soil, planting corn, or driving the tractor.

Sometimes he would take off alone into the desert or the mountains. But Poppa was never alone when he was alone. He passed that on to me. What a great gift!

Sun Valley

Averell Harriman, a friend of my parents and grandparents, founded Sun Valley. A branch of the Union Pacific Railroad, one his family's companies, ended at Ketchum, Idaho, and Harriman was interested in starting a new ski resort, perhaps in that area. As my parents were always looking for a quiet and unspoiled place to get away to, the invitation to see this potential new ski resort way up in the Sawtooth Mountains sounded like a great idea. Averell Harriman and his wife, Marie, were close friends of the Shieldses, and with their encouragement the Coopers ventured to the old town of Ketchum and a one-mile trip up the valley to a place that would come to be called Sun Valley.

Often we drove from Los Angeles to Sun Valley, or sometimes we took the L.A. Super Chief to Salt Lake City and then drove the six-hour journey to Ketchum. It always felt good to head out of Salt Lake, away from the Wasatch mountain range, and to plunge into the flat desert.

Poppa usually drove, and he would heartily recite the poems of Robert W. Service—"The Cremation of Sam McGee," "The Shooting of Dan McGrew"—and all the verses, sung out in full voice to the sagebrush, the cactus, and us, of "Abdul the Bulbul Amir." My mother and I would join in, but nobody would ever have taken that show on the road! The family repertoire also included "Red River Valley," "Ghost Riders in the Sky," "Ol' Man River." Then I would be prodded to deliver "Don't Fence Me In." We laughed a lot.

The time always passed quickly, between our singing, Poppa's bringing things seen in the out-of-doors to our attention, or detouring to do some pistol "plinking" off the side of the road.

One day my father and I went shooting. The highway ran long and completely straight in front of us, some twenty-two miles without a bend. Snow flew, but in spite of that we put tin cans on clumps of sage and fired away. I wanted to learn "shooting from the hip"—now *that* is really a good feeling, when you shoot and the tin can screams through the air from a direct hit.

The whole gang at the dinner table sometime in the early 1940s, from left to right, Coop, Martha Gellhorn, Winston McCrea, Tillie Arnold, Beartracks Williams, Jack Reddish, Rocky, Ernest Hemingway, Nin McCrea, Lloyd Arnold, and an unidentified woman.

Trail Creek Cabin was the place where everyone congregated, a mile or so up the valley from The Lodge. Many a great evening, wild party, and solid good fun happened under its roof.

The Hemingways and the Coopers often wound up an evening with a nightcap at the Club Rio in Ketchum. The year is 1944, so it's likely that between the camaraderie there was probably some serious talk about the war, which was soon to end. (Photograph, Lloyd Arnold)

Poppa, always shy on the dance floor, was a good sport when my mother insisted they go to Arthur Murray's for lessons to learn the newest steps. She was a *great* dancer—she loved it. Here they are at one of the many Trail Creek Cabin parties in Sun Valley, circa 1940. (Photograph, Lloyd Arnold)

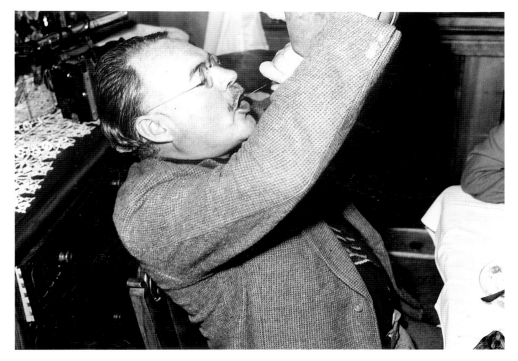

At Trail Creek Cabin, Coop and Ernest, feeling rather happy and competitive, challenge each other in a *bota* (a wine-filled goatskin) drinking contest: How far away can you hold the *bota* and keep a steady stream of wine guided into your mouth? Their admiring audience includes Tillie Arnold and Beartracks.

I'm told that in this contest between the two guys, Ernest was attempting to sing "Lucia" while swallowing wine, and Coop was trying to smoke his cigarette while guzzling his.

Gary Cooper at Trail Creek Cabin, early 1940s, with Darryl Zanuck who
was recovering from an incident on the slopes. Being the head of a studio was
less dangerous. Zanuck and my father shared perfect judgment! Darryl
Zanuck, in 1946: "Video won't be able to hold any market it captures after six
months. People will soon get tired of staring at a plywood box every night."
My father, at a preview of *Gone With the Wind*: "*Gone With the Wind* is
going to be the biggest flop in Hollywood history. I'm just glad it'll be Clark
Gable who'll be falling flat on his face and not Gary Cooper."

These two guys—Gary Cooper and Averell Harriman—
in their "Swiss baggies," mid-1930s, are aliens on the
slopes compared to today's sleek spandex space cadets!

A pretty nifty ski team, from left to right, Rocky,
Patrick Hemingway, Ingrid Bergman, Gary, Clark Gable.
Collectively they looked better than they skied.

Masters of the mountain—Cooper and Gable, with
Siggie Engel at their side. In truth, skiing was much
more of a triumph for my father than anybody realized.
Due to the badly healed broken hip of his childhood, he
could never use the "snowplow" to brake. He had to
learn parallel skiing from day one.

"I ought to knock down the legend that when I'm not acting I'm tongue-tied. I've been described for years as a man whose vocabulary is limited to 'Yup' and 'Nope.' Well, I can bring up reliable witnesses, like Robert Taylor or Ernest Hemingway, who will complain that on hunting and fishing trips I'm so gabby I keep them awake all night." —Gary Cooper, shown here with Gable and Beartracks. (Photograph, Robert Capa)

Beartracks, our wonderful friend and fishing and hunting guide, was part of the Sun Valley family. Here he joins Cooper in some refreshment. (Photograph, Robert Capa)

Picasso and Cooper

It was my mother's initial friendship with David Douglas Duncan, the remarkable photographer, writer, artist, and Marine seen here with my father and Picasso, that opened a rich chapter in our lives. David and his wife, Sheila, truly became extended family for us. David was responsible for introducing two special artists to one another—Pablo Picasso and Gary Cooper. In some of his own books on Picasso, David captured some unique moments as those two men met, sized each other up, and got along splendidly.

It was on our second visit to see Picasso and Jacqueline that my father and mother and I arrived at Villa Californie, Picasso's then home, with Poppa carrying over his arm a "loaded bag," literally so, as it was filled with a six-shooter, bullets, and his white Stetson from *Saratoga Trunk*, as gifts for Pablo.

Once we arrived and had made our greetings, we all moved out to the garden and to a scene I shall never forget. The two men set up paint cans as targets against the palm trees, and fire away they did, while Jacqueline gathered up children and dogs, and we all ran behind some of the large sculptures. My father subtly but deliberately aimed his "wild" shots into the trunk of an old palm tree. In true gentlemanly style, he did not show up his pistol-mate, and deliberately missed many shots. Picasso's accuracy with the brush far exceeded that with the gun, but Poppa was not about to show off.

Now who do you suppose these characters are?
Two kids who loved to play games. Vallauris, 1957.
(Photograph, T. Darvas)

OPPOSITE: David Duncan summed this moment up best
of all: "Gary Cooper . . . brought a gift that thrilled
Picasso—the eagle-feathered warbonnet of an American
Indian chief. Within seconds—masked in a ferocious
scowl above cruel lips, beneath chilling eyes—Pablo,
the master mime, had transformed himself into a haunt-
ing image of that last unbroken warrior who saw the
future, then disappeared into a starless night." Picasso
stuck a bull's tail by his left ear. He looked like Sitting
Bull and he knew it! (Photograph, David Douglas
Duncan, 1957)

Picasso was showing us canvases, lifting one picture after another out of a large stack, showing it, then whisking it away to face the wall. Suddenly, after the paintings of strange-bodied women and obnoxious-looking children, there appeared this rather classic picture of a lady in black—Jacqueline—of such tranquil beauty and strength we all gasped. It's not a very large canvas, but its power dominated the entire huge room. When my father indicated that we were all smitten with *this* painting, Picasso half-smiled and said, "No, no, no. This is a family picture," and whoosh! it vanished back among the wooden stretchers and primed linen.

He did, however, let us choose two paintings that day—another portrait of Jacqueline, a seated profile in an armchair, a woman as patient as time itself, and a studio "interior" for my grandparents Veronica and Paul Shields. We loved our painting but always remembered the *other*. (Photograph, David Douglas Duncan)

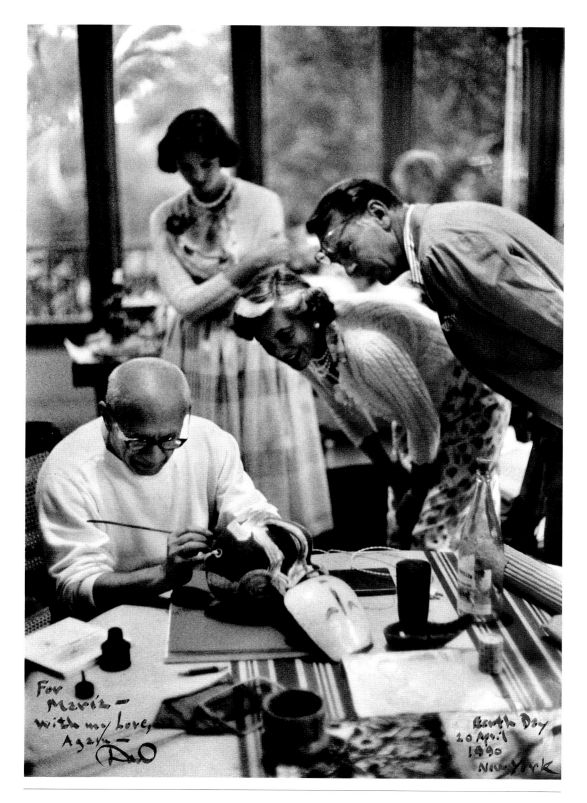

From the expressions on their faces, my parents know this is a magical moment as Picasso paints an inscription to them on the bottom of a ceramic lamp. (Photograph, David Douglas Duncan, 1957)

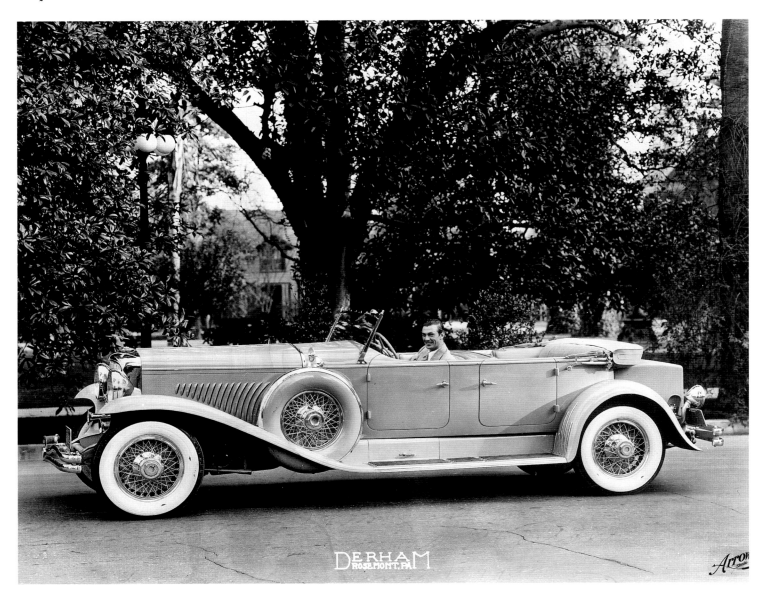

Coop and his Duesenberg, 1920s.

For the Love of Cars

Cars, cars, cars—Cooper loved cars! They were a life-long passion. My father started early to acquire sleek, racy, elegant automobiles, both foreign and domestic, beginning with a chartreuse Duesenberg and moving on to Jaguar and Mercedes-Benz. He flew over to the Mercedes factory in Stuttgart, and spent days with the technicians, exchanging ideas and giving them some suggestions while they worked on his special model. He really enjoyed doing that.

Not only did my father love to drive cars, he knew how to take care of them, and spent countless hours either under the chassis or under the hood, modifying and fine-tuning them himself. No matter the car, he poured himself into its "care and feeding."

Tony Quinn told me that one day Poppa was showing him some new "thing" in a Jaguar he had just gotten, when Peter Lawford stopped by. The car was in the driveway, the hood was up, and Peter started to reach into the guts of the engine. My father stopped him abruptly, saying, "Hey, Pete. You can fiddle with me, you can fiddle with my wife, but you can't fiddle with my car!"

He loved all kinds of cars—sportsters, roadsters, station wagons, convertibles. And he loved the racing look and speed of a car, although on the highway he was a careful driver—in fact, an excellent one—fast, quick reflexes and low tolerance for yahoos on the road who didn't belong there. He taught me how to take corners like the racing drivers do, and he drummed into my head the dangers of sloppy driving, reckless driving, and inattention.

But I think he always harbored a secret desire to have an extremely hot car, take it to the Bonneville Salt Flats near Salt Lake City, and let 'er rip. In his early years, he would take his favorite car of the moment to the Murdoch dry lake bed, where drivers could test their "babies."

Cooper enjoyed horses, and he certainly enjoyed horsepower. In the mid-1950s one of his cars was a Plymouth model with the racy tail fins. He ordered it specially equipped with bucket seats, racing tires, police braking system, and the biggest Chrysler engine they made at the time under its hood—this was a *hot* car! He had it painted a nondescript dusty brown. One day he was sitting at a red light, looking fairly insignificant. Some hot-rod kids spotted "the big movie star" and indicated not too politely they wanted to "drag." He shrugged a meek "okay," hit the accelerator, and that baby took off like a Titan rocket. He had a hell of a lot of fun with that car. Next to the Plymouth in our garage was a beautiful "Sable-and-Sand" Bentley with a Hooper body. As a hood ornament, he placed on it a beautifully designed Lalique crystal eagle's head.

Over time, my parents would go together to major races such as Sebring in Florida and the Monaco Grand Prix to watch their friends race, including famous drivers such as Stirling Moss and Juan Fangio.

This very fast, very cantankerous car was like a
highly tuned thoroughbred. My father gave it extra care
and attention and put additional vents in the hood
to keep it cool.

Answering the cry "Surf's up," we would throw the surfboards in the station wagon to go down to Malibu. My father let Rocky do the honors in this sport. As usual, she was a leader, one of the first to have the new lightweight fiberglass boards. By today's standards of small, sleek double-finned boards, these look like antiques, but they were a far cry from the old ten- and eleven-foot redwood ones used traditionally by native Hawaiians and lifeguards.

Underwater Buddies

My mother launched our family into a new sport, scuba diving. Inspired by Jacques Cousteau, who was funded by our family friend Lowell Guinness, the glorious underwater world opened up to us, and with a little encouragement from fellow actor Eddie Albert, the Coopers made their first dive off the coast of Cap d'Antibes.

With an innocent vanity and total ignorance, my mother and I thought we could keep our hair dry by wearing bathing caps. The teachers didn't tell us stubborn Americans this was a *most dangerous* thing to do. Caps prevent the water from equalizing the pressure inside the ear, and we could have burst our eardrums. As it was, Eddie got a nosebleed, and we were underwater looking at the wondrous sights when we turned to see our friend's mask full of water and blood.

We survived our baptism and Rocky's enthusiasm infected everybody, friends as well. First she found out who was the best. That was one of her knacks, in everything. The Mistral brothers, twins who dove professionally for the city of L.A., came to the house to give us lessons in the pool. After we passed our tests, we struck out early one morning for Redondo Beach, where they met us with a boat, and off we went a mile or so outside the breakwater to dive on the shipwreck of old trolley cars. An enterprising ecologist had dumped them there to make an underwater garden center, a gathering place for sea life to flourish.

Underwater we checked each other's "buddy" and followed Bob Mistral through the unusually clear water. It was cold blue, deep and dense, with shafts of sunlight broken up and sparkling off the little bits of debris that drifted all around us. Out of the gloom suddenly loomed a thing—several "things": the rusted-out streetcars, one of them bearing the name "Desire." Some were on their sides, others straight on rusted wheels. The glass in the windows had long ago vanished and fish, manta rays, sand sharks swam in and out of the empty frames, unconcerned passengers on their silent ride. We hung in total suspension, not moving anything, yet we rose and fell with the tide itself, like a perfectly fitting part of the ocean universe from which we once came.

Another time brought another challenge, night diving—scary as hell!—with a miner's lamp around our heads. Poppa was not for it at all but my mother insisted on proving she could conquer her fear. One unexpected delight that night was the phosphorescence in the water. Whenever we disturbed the waters we left an incredibly beautiful trail of light. A simple stroke of the arm caused a stream of bursting sparks, like a comet sweeping across a night sky.

A Graduation Day of sorts—we are now "certified" divers. (Photograph, Phil Stern)

"Buddies" underwater as well as topside, an alien
couple revel in more of nature's beauties. Nassau, 1960
(Photograph, Bruce Parker)

An optimistic diver. Nassau, 1960 (Photograph, Bruce Parker)

Hollywood Parties

Rocky was the "hostess with the mostest." She knew how to plan parties—how to make them beautiful, delicious, and filled with interesting groups of guests. She followed a few rules of thumb: always have at least one or two extra good-looking gals, and mix people with different areas of interest, especially as neither she nor my father particularly enjoyed people only talking shop.

When I got older, she let me help plan menus, do the seating, and so forth. All was usually well, except for the night I went off to a high school dinner dance of my own, with twenty forgotten place cards left unseated in my bathrobe pocket. She survived the dinnertime chaos, but I sure got hell when I came home! I don't blame her.

My parents would tent-in the terrace and part of the garden with a clear Plexiglas front that would let us see the entire garden down the lawn to the illuminated swimming pool and weeping willow tree. Cooper parties epitomized elegance, beauty, and fun, and invitations to them were eagerly received.

In one of the most famous of all Hollywood pictures, photographer Slim Aarons captured a marvelous moment: New Year's Eve at Romanoff's in the late 1950s.

What is the story behind this shot of the so-called Kings of Hollywood? Slim was describing his big acting debut, in which he had totally blown the only two lines of dialogue he had been given. The story of his disaster completely broke up his more experienced buddies—Clark Gable, Van Heflin, Gary Cooper, and Jimmy Stewart.

DSNE MARTIN
2005
SLIM AARONS

A pasha and his harem girl get ready for a wild night under a tent swagged with rainbow-colored silks, and filled with music and dancing into the early morning. Southampton summers saw many a beautiful dinner party, but few equaled the Fernanda and Donald Leas' Arabian Nights extravaganza. (Photograph, Irving Cantor)

Veteran actor of many fine Westerns, Randolph Scott, with Gary and Rocky, late 1930s. No need to identify the skinny guy in the middle, a very young Mr. Sinatra.

Another Sun Valley New Year's Eve—Norma Shearer, with her racy hat, and Marty Arroge. (Norma's husband, Marty, a great skier, was the first person to steer me down a slope, age five.)

Henry Hathaway, Anne Ford, Richard Burton, and Merle Oberon at a Cooper party given for their close friends from New York, Anne and Henry Ford, in the mid-1950s. (Photograph, Jean Howard)

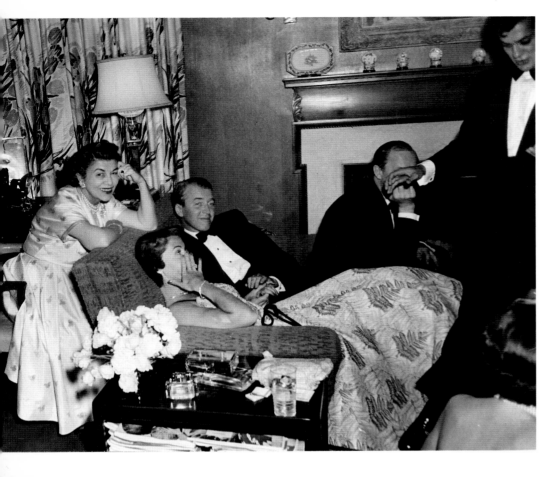

Relaxing in the library after a dinner party at home. My grandmother Veronica Shields, Gloria and Jimmy Stewart, and, in the corner showing a new dance step, Tony Curtis. Tony is cutting a mean rug and has everyone laughing until they cry.

Shortly thereafter, there was almost a catastrophe. One of the guests had gone to my father's room and was looking at a gun Gary had just acquired. He picked it up and brought it into the library, and without checking to see if the barrel was empty, started waving it around. Just as my father roared out, "Damn it! You haven't checked to see if it's empty! Put that down!" the gun went off and tore a hole in the wall right next to the fireplace. The bullet grazed the pants leg of one of the guests. My father was always excruciatingly careful about never having a loaded gun around, but sometimes accidents happen.

Laurence Olivier's prodigious memory impressed and flattered my mother. Six months after an aborted dinner conversation with her, he picked it up exactly where they had left off. (Photograph, Jean Howard)

A young Sammy Davis, Jr., joins the impromptu jamming after dinner. He was then part of a group called the Will Maston Trio. This dinner party, thrown by my parents, was the first time most of their crowd had met or heard Sammy Davis, Jr. This was well before Sinatra or the Rat Pack days. Peter Lawford had simply said to my mother, "Rocky, I want you to meet and hear a terrific talent."

These were the kind of nights that, as it got late, Sinatra or Judy Garland would stand around the piano and begin to sing. Sometimes there was a pianist, but often Judy would simply break into song. I remember as a teenager standing by the dining room door hearing her sing "Danny Boy," with the tears rolling down my cheeks. (Photograph, Jean Howard)

Milton Berle mimicking a Picasso painting, 1958.

Marlene Dietrich in a heartfelt discussion. (Photograph, Jean Howard)

Longtime buddies Edie Goetz (daughter of Louis B. Mayer) and Frank Sinatra. The Goetzes and the Coopers had adjoining properties in Holmby Hills, and Bill and my father went into a couple of joint productions, *They Came to Cordura* being one of them.

Bogie, ahead of his time, sporting an earring just for the hell of it. Paul Shields, my conservative Wall Street grandfather, is enjoying a good laugh. (Photograph, Jean Howard)

Three elegant and beautiful women and very dear family friends—Audrey Hepburn, Connie Wald, Rosalind Russell. By just being there, each in her own special way brought so much kindness and good spirits to any room or event.

Relaxed, delicious dinners at Connie and Jerry Wald's house followed by a screening of some new movie in their library were part of a weekly ritual that the Cooper family always happily looked forward to.

Janet Leigh, Humphrey
Bogart, Molly Dunne.

A New Year's Eve "Make
Your Own Hat" contest. Coop
is declared the winner by
hostess Roz Russell.

When she moved to California after her marriage to Peter Lawford, Pat Kennedy Lawford and my parents became especially close pals. David O. Selznick was producer of, among other things, the immortal *Gone With the Wind*.

Dean Johnson, in so many ways the bedrock of both the Cooper and Stewart families, was introduced to us by Connie and Jerry Wald. Dean is a family lawyer, close friend, and confidant, and a great human being.

Producer Dominick Dunne and his wife, Lennie, waiting with Patrick Rothschild and Kate Smith for the after-dinner jam session to begin.

Movie Time

"The stories of men like Sergeant York and Lou Gehrig, who symbolize and point out not America's faults and failings but her virtues and valor, these are the kind of stories I like to make and hope to go on making." —Gary Cooper

Gary Cooper portrayed the real heroes. He also portrayed the symbolic ones. It's interesting to note that whenever or wherever in the world a national crisis is about to break, *High Noon* cartoons seem to appear in magazines and newspapers. In this film Gary Cooper epitomizes the lone sheriff in man's classic confrontation between good and evil.

Always unassuming in his ways, my father lived his belief that he was "an average Charlie who became a movie star." The milieu of his daily work life became the soundstage and locations God knows where, from a pitching, rolling aircraft carrier to Death Valley; from a canyon in the Mexican hills to the Place de la Concorde and the Ritz Hotel in Paris; from Apia, Western Samoa, to a Montana mountain pass in a blizzard. He enjoyed location work and the adventure of being in a new place, even if the recreation was limited to a local bar. Work was hard, tedious, and at times lonely. In the early days of filmmaking, the one day off, Sunday, was eagerly anticipated. Here's a letter written to my mother in 1942 while on location in Sonora Pass shooting *For Whom the Bell Tolls:*

July 2, Thursday
My dearest,

I'm surely missing you a lot, and I think it's because six weeks seems such a hell of a long time from now.

As for me, the trip up here was quite nice. Beautiful weather and scenery. Got here for lunch, established myself in the cabin, which is all right, have a living room, kitchen, bedroom, a decent shower, and a large porch overlooking a roaring river of white water. The trees are enormous pines and redwoods.

We put in a full day today. Started shooting at eight, got back to camp at six-thirty—dinner—it's now nine o'clock and I can tell nightlife will consist of brushing zee teeth and going to bed. I shall take lots of movies, as the country is really enormous, rugged, and beautiful. The camp is about six thousand feet, and the location today up over nine thousand. My wind must be pretty good because I seem to puff and snort much less than anyone else. Well, my angel, I hope you feel as well as I do, and miss me as much as I do you. Tell Cakes to be a good girl and that her Poppa loves her and her mama more than anything else in the world. XXXXX

My father made close to a hundred films, including silents and two-reelers. His start was in Westerns, but his looks and way with the camera and women expanded his territory, so by the late twenties and early thirties Gary Cooper was a "hell-bent-for-leather ridin'-shootin' cowboy" in one picture, and in the next a debonair, suave romantic in top hat and tails. He could be all charm and seduction in one type of role *(Desire, Design for Living, Bluebeard's Eighth Wife),* switch to a Foreign Legion adventurer-type *(Lives of a Bengal Lancer),* or portray real-life heroes like Sergeant York and Lou Gehrig. It's not surprising that the public saw Gary Cooper as the embodiment of dreams. He was America's Everyman in the great Frank Capra films *Mr. Deeds Goes to Town* and *Meet John Doe.* In those pictures he exposed his own vulnerability and endeared himself to all. No resume of my father's life—personal or professional—would be complete without mention of director Henry Hathaway, who was a close colleague and family friend. My father did six films with Henry, including *Lives of a Bengal Lancer* (1935), which won six Academy Award nominations.

Movies are a weird mixture of illusion and reality. Poppa never held forth much about acting. He commented on it rarely, but lots was going on behind the impression he gave of doing nothing.

My father once said, "The general consensus seems to be that I don't act at all. I like the story, recently attributed to Akim Tamiroff, with whom I worked in *The General Died at Dawn* and *For Whom the Bell Tolls*. Tamiroff got his early training in the Moscow Art Theater, and according to the story he had been warned that in my quiet way I might emerge from a scene looking better than he did. For three days we had worked together without seeing any rushes, but at last they came in.

"After seeing them, Akim is quoted as saying, 'For three days I've acted rings around him. I've got him stopped. Against my acting, he can do nawthing. I have every scene. So I look at the rushes. On the screen, I am there. Everybody else is there. But what do I see? Nawthing! Nawthing, that is, but Gary Cooper.'"

My father always said, "If I know what I'm doing, I don't have to act."

Director Marion Gering, while working on a scene with Cooper and Tallulah Bankhead, once yelled at him, "Mr. Cooper, will you now begin to act?" Charles Laughton roared back, "He is acting, you idiot. Only you don't see it. The camera does." Another time Laughton said, "I knew in a flash Gary had something I should never have. It is something pure and he doesn't know it's there. In truth, that boy hasn't the least idea how well he acts."

My father's description of how an actor prepares shows that things were not left to chance on his part. Around 1924 or 1925, he embraced the idea of acting quite seriously and experimented at home with facial expressions and makeup. In his words:

Beautiful, adorable, *real* Audrey Hepburn. Poppa loved her. We all love her still. He was once asked his reaction to making love before the camera. His answer was: "Well, everything you do before the camera is work—some is nice work, some is just *work*." Obviously working with Audrey was *very* nice work, seen here in *Love in the Afternoon*.

"I resolved that by some means I would learn to act. Having made the decision, I bought a makeup kit, first spying around the drugstore to make sure that no friend witnessed the crack-up of my manhood.

"In those days there was nothing subtle about makeup for western movies. The main idea was to strive for plenty of contrast—chalk-white face powder, heavy lipstick and coal-black mascara. I practiced at home. I'd apply the stuff, and then rush out into the back yard, where my mother would take snapshots of my assorted grimaces. She was an expert amateur photographer, and she did her own darkroom work, so I didn't have to wait long for my daily rushes. Looking at them, I noticed a peculiar thing. The more ferociously I scowled, the funnier I looked. On the other hand, if I just looked at the camera impassively, and thought to myself, *You treacherous little box, if you don't make this one good, I'm going to tear you apart with my two hands, rip out the film and jump on you until you are pulp,* the picture of me would come out looking so mean I'd be shocked."

In that same interview, a memoir for *The Saturday Evening Post* in 1956, he said, "I am not what actors call 'an easy study.' I have to work hard to prepare myself for every scene—so hard that sometimes I have exhausted myself before getting in front of the camera. Working on *His Woman,* I found that the only way I could keep going was to stretch out on a pile of old scenery or anything that was handy, and take a nap between takes. It worked so well that it's still my habit. When I have got myself in character, and have worked over a scene until it's fixed in my mind, I no longer stew around while awaiting the director's call. I just go to sleep.

"I remember one time I nearly overdid the napping during a remake of the old silent classic, *Beau Geste,* in 1938. Most of us had been killed off defending our Foreign Legion fort, and the time had come for the survivors to cremate us in the ruins. Robert Preston had the job of carrying me in and stretching me out on my bunk, after which he drenched the room with oil.

"'Now don't go to sleep,' he warned. 'We're going to set fire to this place in a minute.'

"'But if you do go to sleep,' warned the director, 'don't snore and ruin the sound track.'

"He got his shot of me on the bed, and went away. I knew a lot of time would be wasted before they got around to burning up the set. Everything would have to be set up perfectly, because there could be no retakes. So I went sound asleep.

"In the general excitement before the conflagration, I was forgotten. The fire was pretty well along before Preston hollered, "Great day, where's Coop?" He charged into the flames just about the time I began to dream I was back on the set of *I Take This Woman.* Fortunately, I wake up easily. Preston and I came smoking out of the room so fast the cameraman thought the set had exploded, and I've never been able to sleep through a fire scene since."

Even in the last weeks of his life, only once did I ever hear him discuss his profession, and one day he said very simply, but with a great deal of irritation, "Damn! Just when I was beginning to understand a little what acting is all about." This, from the man about whom Stanislavsky and Charles Laughton said he knew more about acting than anybody.

It's interesting how, through movies, the public can identify with and come to know as real a Longfellow Deeds, a John Doe, a Sheriff Will Kane. These characters take on lives of their own, and become elements in our personal and national character.

One of Cooper's first films, about 1925, was a five-reeler titled *Tricks.* In the photo shown here, he is on the extreme left, wearing an outlandishly big Western hat, along with J. Frank Glendon and Marilyn Mills. The picture was a real "horse opera." His pay for this great epic was ten dollars a day.

In 1926, Henry King, one of the major directors at Goldwyn Studios, eased Cooper into his "big role" in *The Winning of Barbara Worth.* The actor originally hired for the part was delayed in another film, and King's time and budget were running out. My father recalls:

"'You're as tall and skinny as Harold Goodwin,' he said to me. 'If you still think you can act, I'll let you double for him on the long shots. O.K.?'

"I was shaky, but I made good background. Then I was called on for medium-long shots. These, too, seemed to pass inspection. Still no Goodwin.

"Two important studio scenes remained to be shot before the company moved to location in Nevada. One called for Goodwin to lurch into Colman's frontier hotel room after a desperate eighty-mile ride, and blurt out his message of disaster. King figured that with enough dust on my face after the eighty miles across the desert, he would be safe in using me as a double. But I couldn't seem to raise enough sweat to get dusty, and I never managed to look exhausted. After fifteen or twenty rehearsals and a dozen takes in front of the camera, I could look tired, but not bone-dry tired.

"So one morning King started running me around the studio at seven A.M. An hour later I was showing signs of strain, but he reminded me of the Marathon racers, and for art's sake, I kept on going. After about ten miles of this, he'd meet me about every fourth round and throw dust in my face. When I didn't seem to be sweating to

his satisfaction, he'd haul out a spray gun and settle the dust with a film of water. By the time he decided I looked exhausted enough, I was staggering, completely done in. He caught me as I came around, steered me onto the set in front of the cameras, and said, 'Give 'em the message.'

"The lights and the heat hit me full in the face. I opened my mouth mechanically, saw the camera spinning around me, and fell flat. Colman caught my head just before it hit the floor. Sam Goldwyn, who was watching, said it was the finest bit of acting he had seen up to that point. So who am I to deny it?"

The comments about Gary Cooper's "natural" acting talents are true. However, his powers of observation as an artist also stood him in good stead, and, to quote him directly, "During the making of *Beau Sabreur* I added William Powell to the list of talented performers who were giving me hints on how the acting business should be conducted. When I read somewhere that I am a natural-talent boy who never had an acting lesson in his life, I wonder what all those thousands of hours add up to that I spent with Ronald Colman, Bill Powell, John Huston, Henry King, Sam Goldwyn, Cecil B. DeMille, Charles Laughton, Thelma Todd, Claudette Colbert, Helen Hayes, Marlene Dietrich, Barbara Stanwyck—the list runs on and on. If those weren't lessons conducted under the most competitive of professional circumstances, then I wouldn't know a lesson if I saw one."

Luckier than many actors, Gary Cooper smoothly made the transition from silent films to talkies—"As a veteran hog and cattle caller, I could bellow loud enough to knock the earphones off the sound engineer."

Doing his own stunt riding in scenes like these from 1938 showed what a fantastic horseman Cooper was. The physical strength needed for feats like this was one of the reasons he'd spend regular hours working out at home.

Those were not the days of a "personal trainer," so my father went to his weights, and to two boxer's punching bags, a five-foot one and a smaller fast one that was hanging in our outdoor dog kennel. Gloves on, he'd work up quite a sweat with lightning-fast jabs and power punches. He took some time out showing me the ladylike art of self-defense—from working out with child-size boxing gloves to the "Irish knee." I loved it!

This was the great Cecil B. DeMille's first film with Gary Cooper. My father, playing the role of Wild Bill Hickock, was funny and fierce. These are the last three shots of a nine-frame sequence from *The Plainsman* (1936). The completed action, from holstered gun to drawn and fired—at the target, not one's own foot!—is one-third of a second. Very fast!

This act of violence registering on the human face, transforming it into that of a wild primitive animal, is awesome to see, frozen in bloodless moments of pure anger and deadly action. It's only a movie, but. . . . In this movie, the character of Wild Bill Hickock was fascinating for my father, and, as he said later:

"I was always conscious of the influence of the character I was playing. Whether the character was real or fictional, I would read everything I could find about his life and times. To prepare myself for such Westerns as *The Plainsman, The Westerner, High Noon,* and some dozen others, I have read just about everything on the West that's worth reading, fact or fiction. I make the same preparation if I'm given a military role, or a scientific role, or the role of a Quaker farmer caught up in the Civil War. By the time I get before the camera, Cooper has less to say about the way he acts than the character he has become."

Speaking of character, Cooper showed his own during one episode on location in Montana. Filming *The Plainsman,* the whole crew got snowed in, quite far away from the supply tent; the stars, however, were put up in more comfortable and better-equipped quarters. Late at night, my father made himself up as an Indian and joined all the extras on a raid of the commissary to get more food and refreshments for the rest of the crew. This was in the days before the unions existed, but my father was true to the image of fighting for the less-privileged guy and he had fun doing it.

On the set of *The Westerner,* four guys wait
for one of those "HOME COOKED MEALS"
advertised on the shingle.

Shot from the set of *The Westerner* (1940). My father sat a horse like glue. It drove him crazy the way many people rode with a heavy rein, constantly "riding the bit," pulling on the horse's mouth and cutting it to pieces. He taught me about being sensitive to the animal, to feel, to command with a squeeze of the knees, and never spur unless absolutely necessary.

He didn't think horses were all that bright in general, but he had great affection for them anyway, and he admired the "smarts" in the horses they used for cutting animals, roping, and doing other ranch work.

Gary Cooper as Sergeant York (1941). This is the role that won my father his first Oscar. As my father once said about this role, "It took everything I had and I gave it everything I had." Or, to quote one of York's real-life friends, Cooper's "the spittin' image of Alvin."

My father spoke of playing the role of Sergeant Alvin York in the following way:

"I remember my first big struggle with my responsibility to the movie-going public. Hal Wallis showed me a script called Sergeant York, based on the real-life story of the great hero of World War I. In screen biographies dealing with remote historic characters, some romantic leeway is permissible. But York happened to be very much alive, his exploits were real, and I felt that I couldn't do justice to him. York himself came to tell me I was his own choice for the role, but I still felt I couldn't handle it. Here was a pious, sincere man, a conscientious objector to war, who, when called, became a heroic fighter for his country. He was too big for me. He covered too much territory.

"To prepare myself for the role, I visited Sergeant Alvin C. York in his own Tennessee hills and absorbed from his faith and philosophy. He didn't smoke or drink or swear, and he believed that every man had a right to live in peace. But the more he prayed for guidance, the clearer it became that peace could not be preserved by meek surrender to an aggressor. Once convinced that it was up to the strong to resist attacks on the weak, he prayed for strength and became the fightingest soldier in the AEF."

Real-Life Heroes

Lieutenant James Stewart presents his buddy with an Oscar in 1942 for *Sergeant York*. Nineteen years later, with my father too ill to attend the Academy Awards, Jimmy Stewart held Poppa's Honorary Oscar for "many memorable screen performances," accepting it for him on TV and saying, "We're all proud of you, Coop. We're all so very proud." Jimmy started to break down, and that was the first that the public knew that "Coop" was getting ready for his last ride home.

Gary Cooper as Lou Gehrig and Babe Ruth as himself
having batting practice on the set of *The Pride of the
Yankees.*

Training to be Lou Gehrig was not easy. My father used every occasion to practice. Yankee catcher Bill Dickey even came up to Sun Valley, where our family was vacationing, and continued his coaching work with Coop. It was harder than he realized, and my father said:

"I discovered, to my private horror, that I couldn't throw a ball. The countless falls I had taken as a trick rider had so ruined my right shoulder that I couldn't raise my arm above my head.

"Lefty O'Doul, later manager of the Oakland ball club, came down to help me out. 'You throw a ball,' he told me after studying my unique style, 'like an old woman tossing a hot biscuit.' But we went to work, and after some painful weeks he got my arm to working in a reasonable duplication of Gehrig's throw. There remained one outstanding difference. Gehrig was a southpaw, and I threw right-handed."

They finally succumbed to the impossibility of my father's being able to hit left-handed and ingeniously shot those sequences normally and then reversed the film. Of course, that required any and all letters, numbers, or signs that might show up in the background to be written backward, so that on film it would look normal. Even the numbers on the uniforms had to be sewn on in reverse.

Ingrid Bergman said about my father:
"You never noticed that he was working. He spoke quietly, never tried to do an interpretation like Alec Guinness. Instead he did little things with his face and his hands, little things you didn't even know were there until you saw the rushes and realized how tremendously effective he was. . . ." Here the two stars meet for lunch at the Brown Derby, 1945.

OPPOSITE: In *For Whom the Bell Tolls* (1943) the coming together of Hemingway's character Robert Jordan and Gary Cooper seemed to be a perfect fit, seen here with Ingrid Bergman and Katina Paxinou.

Gary Cooper on the steps of the Capitol in Washington, D.C., on location filming *The Court Martial of Billy Mitchell,* 1955. "Who is Billy Mitchell?" most would ask. Only the brigadier general of the Army Air Service who tried to convince the army and navy of the importance of air power for our defense. The time: right after World War I. The result: for his beliefs and for telling the truth, court-martial. Again Cooper takes on a role probing the sources of a man's inner character and convictions, and sticking to the truth no matter the cost.

Waiting for a scene. My father felt that in his responsibility to the public, he was a composite of all the figures that he played. He always wondered, "What did this composite look like? Who was he? And how could he be responsible for him?" (Photograph, Don Ornitz)

Grace Kelly, the newcomer on the scene at the time of *High Noon*, is shown between takes with my father and Lloyd Bridges.

OPPOSITE: While on location for *High Noon*, Grace Kelly's hat seems to be the only shade around on a hot sunny day. Of this major role in his career, my father said:

"When Stanley Kramer sent me the script, I saw in it a graphic presentation of everything Dad had taught me at home. As a trial lawyer and later a judge in the Montana Supreme Court, Dad knew sheriffs all over the West, and he knew what they were up against. Law enforcement, as he taught it to me, was everybody's job. The sheriff was not a lone figure, but the representative of the people's desire for law and order, and unless he had the people behind him, he was in poor shape. Such a man was the sheriff I was asked to portray."

They Came to Cordura (1959), which delved into the issue of what defines a real hero, deeply intrigued my father. The story's exploration of man's own fears, self-doubts, and redemption was continually Cooper's challenge. Major Thomas Thorn, a man accused of cowardice in battle, is to lead a group of "heroes" to where they can be duly honored. On that journey, the men's true characters come out, and who is really a hero becomes revealed. (Photograph, Coburn, Jr.)

A shot from *The Hanging Tree* (1959)—or—from life?
Where is Poppa looking?—Toward the future? The past?
Inward? I don't know. (Photograph, Willard Hatch)

"The Last Performance"

During a falconing demonstration, a trained golden eagle was brought to Dollar Mountain. The trainer put a strong leather sheath around my father's forearm, and when Poppa thrust his leather-cuffed wrist forward, 13 pounds of golden eagle flew in, landed, and fiercely eyeballed him. This was his bird, his spirit source. The intensity of that encounter momentarily overrode the pain my father was having in his neck and shoulders—the cancer that would cut short his own flight was starting to do its dirty work. But on this afternoon in Sun Valley, 1961, in a snow-filled meadow, it was only a mighty man and a mighty bird that counted.

Donald Hyatt, the renowned producer of such TV series as NBC's *Project Twenty* and *Victory at Sea,* was producer/director for the last film my father ever made, a marvelous documentary called *The Real West.* Gary Cooper was never a crusader, but his passion for the American Indian, his anger and sorrow at what we, the United States, did to their great nation and culture, ran strong in his veins until his last day. *Nothing* was going to stop him from contributing to this documentary.

Mr. Hyatt, shown opposite at left along with screenwriter Phillip Reisman, gives a vibrant and accurate portrait of Gary Cooper in his article "The Last Performance," written for *Variety* in 1961:

Every once in a great while some event occurs, some good fortune happens, some person comes into your life with such force that the experience becomes a part of your thinking and your working . . . from then on.

Gary Cooper was such a person and working with him was such an event. Those who knew him were fortunate. No one of us who worked with him during that last year will ever forget the experience. Everything that was Gary Cooper seemed to be in sharper focus during those days last March as we watched him give his last performance—great as an actor, greater as a human being.

It was a little over a year ago when Jerry Wald suggested that we talk to Gary Cooper about a "Project Twenty" show which we were planning and for which we were seeking a storyteller. We called it *The Real West,* and Jerry said that there could never be a title and subject more tailored to "Coop's" interests. A few days later Gary called, and taking no chance that my production team and I had ever heard of him, introduced himself and asked if he could come by for a "minute." He had a way of making things refreshingly simple and direct.

That visit lasted four hours while he shuffled through hundreds of photographs we had collected on those early days of the West. Before he laid the first picture down, you knew that Gary really did love the old West. He talked of how he had been a part of it as a cowhand on his father's Montana ranch, and what it was like to grow up with a cowpony under you. But it became apparent that it was the people of the West he loved the most—"real people" he called them.

Through many afternoons, it was the people of the old West we talked about—the Indians, the sodbusters, the cattlemen, the gold-seekers—all of those people who took part in that grand American adventure. Gary would go through the old daguerreotypes and carefully study the faces, wondering what kind of person this or that one was, and why they went West. "Look at this old boy here—I'll bet he pushed the wagon West himself—swearing all the way!"

When it came to the miners, he viewed them with plain envy—feeling that he'd missed out on the fun of scratching up, down and over the virgin West with a pick and pan. The miner represented that free and independent spirit of the old West he admired most—and the downright excitement of looking for gold (never mind if you found it) had a great appeal to him.

Indian Expert

Of our hundred-odd daguerreotypes of Indians, Gary knew most of them by name and tribe. If they had figured in the Indian Wars he generally knew the when and where of that particular battle. He felt that those frozen expressions had an unmatched beauty about them. As a youth he had made many Indian friends on the nearby Flathead Reservation.

Chief Joseph was one of his favorites, and I guess it was appropriate that the last words Gary Cooper ever spoke professionally were those of Chief Joseph speaking at the end of the Indian Wars. *"Hear me, my chiefs. I am tired. My heart is sad and sick. From where the sun now stands I will fight no more . . . forever."*

When Gary Cooper finished those lines of *The Real West*, he went to bed, and seven weeks later he had gone.

When he came to New York on March 19 to finish his work on *The Real West*, he wasn't feeling well, and he couldn't hide it. "Acute arthritis in the neck," he called it apologetically. He would matter-of-factly rub his neck and only once conceded it was "sort of a bother." He was unable to work for very long periods of time, and he became concerned—not about himself, but his slower working pace. He thought he might be a financial burden on the show, and that too many people were kept waiting for him. He was even concerned that we might think he was showing actor's temperament. "Hope you don't think I'm one of those fellows," he said.

No one will ever know what it took out of Gary to get through those days—the sweat was always visible. But what he gave to those around him will never be forgotten . . . his boyish enthusiasm for his first big venture in television and his genuine modesty in doing it . . . his patience and desire to do lines over again and again . . . his sense of humor which could even blossom under tension and pain . . . his wonderful selflessness.

Working with Gary became more than a professional relationship. It was a human experience . . . an unforgettable one.

When Gary died on May 13, it wasn't surprising to find that his loss was deeply felt throughout the world. During his 35 years as an actor, he characterized a rich human spirit. Gary Cooper personified that in real life, and never more so than in that last year. His greatness was his infinite love of people.

End Time

Poppa, what were you thinking, remembering, dreaming, hoping, praying? Is this a picture of Gary Cooper or Sergeant York or Lou Gehrig or Sheriff Will Kane or John Doe? Is it a picture of Longfellow Deeds, Mr. Flanagan, or Robert Jordan? Or is it Joe Average American standing on a brink, looking far, dreaming tall, and wanting to embody all of the above?

It's you, Poppa, who felt you always wanted to portray the best a man could be in your professional roles, and who struggled and wondered how to live that in real life. (Photograph, Earl Thiesen, 1957)

The year 1957 took my father back to some of the places that had meaning in his early life. He roamed the hills and rocks of his childhood, revisited Yellowstone, and checked in with new friends like Bill Studdard, owner of the Gang Ranch, a humongous hunk of land that spread over Montana and into Canada.

Some intriguing film offers came along, and Poppa enjoyed using his newly acquired scuba diving skills in a sea adventure, *The Wreck of the Mary Deare*, with Charlton Heston. In *The Hanging Tree*, he had a great time working in Yakima, Washington, with Delmar Daves as the director and Maria Schell his co-star. But a picture he never got to make really had him turned on— both the story and the opportunity to work again with his special friend Fred Zinnemann. It was a film called *The Sundowners*, and was to be shot in Australia. Timing was bad! While they were in negotiations, the cancer that was to terminate his life first showed itself, and after initial surgery, doctors and everyone felt a rough location in the outback was not called for. My father was deeply disappointed. His colleague Robert Mitchum and Deborah Kerr did the honors.

In the mid to late fifties, my father's conversion to Catholicism started silently. He never discussed much about it but simply started joining us for Mass more often. The ostensible reason was to hear the good sermons given by a dynamic young priest, Father Harold Ford, dubbed by my father as "Father Tough Stuff." Father Ford didn't give hellfire and brimstone, but he was a very human and with-it man. My mother invited him over for a drink one afternoon, thinking there might be some deep and profound conversations about matters of the spirit. Think again! He and my father disappeared into the gun room and as far as I can tell all they talked about was hunting, fishing, and scuba diving. Father Ford became a scuba buddy and joined us diving in the large marineland of the Pacific tank where we all cavorted with its inhabitants.

My father's search for his own spiritual kingdom apparently was coming together, and after many months of learning the basics with Father Ford, and "living with the questions," he did, as Rilke so beautifully put it, "live the questions now. Perhaps then someday far in the future you will gradually, without even knowing it, live your way into the answer." Into the answer he took himself. Shirley Burden, an old and dear friend, himself a convert, was godfather at Poppa's baptism.

And, in a strange irony, Thomas Merton, the inspired, spiritual Trappist monk from the Abbey of Gethsemane, whom he had never met, played an important part in my father's last weeks. Reading Merton's book *No Man Is an Island,* gave Poppa great solace and comfort, and I received a treasured note from Father Louis (Merton) several months later:

October 11, 1961
Dear Maria,

I was touched by your kind letter, and glad that it gives me an opportunity to greet you and your mother personally, and advise you of my friendship and good wishes. With everyone else, I loved Gary Cooper and his great movies, which I often remember with satisfaction—well, relatively often. For it is a long time since I have been to a movie. I even had a temptation and hope that if the *Seven Story Mountain* became a film, he would play in it. This was a clear case of vanity on my part!! Anyway, with all my blessings and good wishes,

Father Louis Merton

P.S. I am sending a book you might like.

My father was still well at the time of his becoming a Catholic. His reasons for converting are his to know. He did say to Hemingway toward the end, "You know, that decision I made was the right one." I know he and Papa spoke about "the Catholic thing." Whatever Ernest's ambivalence was, the two guys obviously hashed out a lot in that area. How tragic that Hemingway's illness had robbed him of the comfort and sense of the supporting arms of God.

Fame, success, sophistication, age—Poppa never lost certain childlike qualities. He kept a fresh eye, sense of play, and couldn't have cared less about looking silly (in the appropriate context).

There was always a mischievous boy changing places with the glamorous romantic leading man. He could be skipping stones on the water or dropping flower petals down a young beautiful lady's dress—a couple of whiskeys probably helped with that game! I understand that whatever happened, there was always an innocence, even in romantic situations that tangled up people's lives for a while, and he always got worked into a lather about ever hurting anyone.

This return to his old Gallatin, Montana, schoolyard playground seems a good place to collapse the years and see him spin and laugh with his young playmates. (Photograph, Earl Thiesen)

My father meeting with his grade school teacher, Ida Davis, after almost fifty years, in Helena. I wish I could have heard what he and Ida talked about during this visit. I know from other photos he brought her flowers, arranged them for her in her little kitchen, and took her to a local restaurant for lunch. (Photograph, Earl Thiesen)

After my father's first surgery for cancer, we returned to the south of France. These are notations from my journal at the time:

"How relaxed we are once we're in the cabana. A darn cold wind, but warm on the pads that have been soaking up the September sun. Did some exercise, and we all warmed up and plunged into the sea.

"The smell of the sage is very strong, and a good wind sound roaring through the pine trees . . . water is 70° and quite a surge from the storm that's moving in. Black, white, blue clouds still building up over the mountains, in the direction of Marseilles. Momma called David Duncan and he put Pablo [Picasso] on—Momma is in the phone booth now stamping her feet . . . no cigarette, no drink—and she's *very* nervous in speaking to P.P. They were leaving for Arles but asked us to come over for a couple of hours. Off we go!

"Such a wonderful and warm greeting from Picasso and Jacqueline. They remembered my grandmother [Mutta] with great affection and said how much she had given of herself when we all visited last year. Momma and I both felt her presence *so* strongly . . . like she was walking with us.

"To be here again is like having time actually turn itself back, and you are doing again something that was so perfect before, and this second time it is too. I don't think people are allowed this privilege very often . . . and maybe this second time is better, more appreciated, because of the bad that preceded it."

We headed up to Paris for some more French R&R. The day of my twenty-fourth birthday, September 15, started at the Plaza Athénée with my mother and father pushing a room service table that held my birthday presents. My journal reflects the day:

"8:30 A.M.—Surprise time! On top of some other gifts, an unbelievably long and beautiful pheasant feather from Poppa. But the real gift was us being together. Lunch at the Ritz with Alice Topping. Dinner at the Windsors'—everything more beautiful even than the last time we were there. A massive arrangement of sunflowers on the gilt mirrored hall table—incredible.

"At the end of dinner, they presented me with a birthday cake. The Duke stood and gave me a charming toast—funny, the last time we were there, it was *his* birthday. The Guinnesses, Gloria and Lowell, Gloria holding forth on Maria Callas; while Elsa Maxwell is sitting across the table, Gloria egging her on—what a witchy conversation.

"When the women went upstairs for coffee, my mother was fascinated to see in the Duchess's bedroom a small needlepoint pillow that had been made by a friend and given to the Duchess. The quotation read:

"My friend with thee to live alone
Methinks 'tis better than to own—
A crown, a sceptre, or a throne."

In January of 1961, the Friars Club honored Gary Cooper with an affectionate roast. The dais was star-studded. Here's my father with Audrey Hepburn, Governor Pat Brown of California, Jack Benny, and Carl Sandburg.

Between the happiness of Christmas and New Year, 1961, a cement cloud crossed the sun. My mother and I were told by our family doctor—Rex Kennemer—that my father's cancer of last year had returned, was inoperable, and that at the most he had six months to live. We didn't tell him right away. He was still feeling pretty well, and Rex said not to let bad news spoil the good, pain-free days that were left. So we went through New Year's Eve, the Friar's Club tribute to my father, and daily life as normal, except that for us each moment was loaded, poignant, so damn precious, and we both felt guilty at keeping the truth from him.

We made our traditional family trip up to Sun Valley in mid-January of 1961. "The girls" skied, Poppa hunted and spent a lot of time out in the low country alone. In my heart, I think he knew, but he never said a word to us, even when bad neck pain started, and Dr. George Saviers, Papa H's doctor, gave him medication.

One day my father did not go down to the low country for hunting, and we did not ski. Instead, the three of us drove up into the pass high in the mountains above Galena. I recorded that afternoon in January 1961 and the following days, in my journal:

"We parked the car, walked along the road, and then cut into the meadows of deep, unbroken snow. The only sound we heard was a woodpecker's call and the wind in the trees. There was no sign of civilization around anywhere, except for an abandoned trapper's cabin stocked with a few emergency supplies. We went inside. We left some peanuts there and then Poppa wrote a message on the wall, and signed it. We laughed at the surprise of a future reader, and went outside to catch the last bit of cool sunlight before blue-shadow time started.

"We walked, talked about nothing in particular, watched a storm coming in, and were very happy. It was a moment in time—a precious short time—but we didn't dwell on that 'clock.' I caught the smiles and the love.

"Later that day we watched horse races on the snow, Ben-Hur style, and on the way home tried to find the gravestone that Hemingway had written on, for our old pal Beartracks. We crisscrossed the graveyard, but couldn't find it."

And again from my journal:

"Sunday again, and Poppa watched us ski down the last part of Warm Springs. We went again to the graveyard, and this time found Beartracks's stone, and right in back of it, Nin's first husband [Gene Van Gelder], with Papa H's inscription on the stone. It was all white, covered and mounded smooth. The three of us, knee-deep in the snow, bent over and dug away the ice crystals down to the rock where the plaque was, with Papa H's words,

> He has come back to the hills that he loved,
> And now he will be part of them forever.

We stand and read that. The jazz and rock and roll music from the "Kinderhorn," the kids' little skiing hill, was in the air. Quite moving that scene! 'What a happy place for a graveyard,' Poppa said. 'With the kids playing and laughing and falling and skiing right next to it.'"

From my journal:

"Monday. Papa Hemingway came back. We went up for a drink at 6:30. It was not indigo night yet, driving from the valley, but as we drove the sky deepened and one star came out. The gate was open this time, and a few car tracks in the old snow still looked new. Came in the kitchen door, Mary greeted us, then Papa came down the stairs—down to 176 pounds, no belly, and new holes punched into the belt. Doctor George Saviers came in. We all had good talk. When we left, Papa, Poppa, Momma and I stood very close in the narrow hall. Poppa said that we had gone to the grave yesterday, and how beautiful the inscription was. Momma said, 'I hope you'll do it for us,' and there was a quiet, and then a mumbling from Ernest that said everything.

"We walked outside, and Papa swung around and grabbed my Poppa, and in that cold dark, two men embraced each other and only the trees and the night and three people who know something very sad witnessed the good-bye. And who knows, especially now, if it is the last time?"

It was. When my father was eventually told the bad news that his cancer had returned, his response was, "We'll pray for a miracle; but if not, and that's God's will, that's all right too."

He was touched by the beautiful wishes of so many fans and friends. One telegram in particular moved him greatly: "Sorry to hear of your illness. You have my prayers and sympathy for your speedy recovery. Your friend and comrade, Sergeant Alvin C. York." Others, too, which arrived during his illness, or just after he died, spoke volumes: "We loved him as if he had been from our own country. Courage, dear madam. Maurice Chevalier"; "The Babe valued your friendship highly. I know he would join me in hope and prayer for your well-being. Clair Ruth"; and, "Your many admirers pray for your recovery and good health. The pleasure you provide millions in your distinguished career makes you a symbol of kindness and strength. As an outstanding ambassador of good will for your country, America has in you a true son winning for it friends from all over the world. Abba Eben, Minister of Education and Culture, Israel."

Cooper and Hemingway, Hemingway house in Ketchum, 1961

It came too soon for all of us—his wife, his daughter, his friends and fans. One day in February 1961 my mother said, in a matter-of-fact way, "We should have a last good family portrait taken." We all knew our time together was limited. She arranged the sitting to be done at home so as to disrupt Poppa as little as possible. We put on a happy face, a mask for then, yes; but in reflecting thanks for the wondrous past— the truth. (Photograph, Johnny Engstead)

Saying Good-bye

My father was initially buried at Holy Cross Cemetery in Santa Monica. The three of us went to choose the plot one day—as Poppa put it, "Well, we'd better go out and buy some real estate!" He chose this particular place between a pine tree (obvious reason) and a fig tree—"I love figs!"—and a view of the airport. "Planes taking off and landing. I like that," he indicated.

In this photo, his mother, Alice Cooper, is supported by her son Arthur and Hazel Gibbons, Uncle Cedric's wife. Howard Cooper, Poppa's nephew, is next to Hazel, and our dear diving buddy, Father Ford, is in the background. (Photograph, Paul Slade)

Among the hundreds who came to say good-bye were Don Robinson, Dolores Hart, Rosalind Russell, and Freddie Brisson.

Some years later, after my mother and I had moved east to New York and Long Island, we also moved my father's coffin to Southampton. There was no family left in L.A., and this place was also home for him. The reburial was quiet and simple. The escort for the hearse was Catenea's Fish Market delivery truck accompanying a few close friends. Appropriate, as Poppa devoured more lobsters and clams from there in a summer than most of us do in a lifetime.

Gary Cooper took a lot of people with him on his life's journey from the hills of Montana to a quiet plot marked with a huge boulder from a Montauk Point rock quarry. The church had some "rules" about why they would not allow that stone in the cemetery, but my mother flashed her green eyes at the presiding pastor and snorted, "Do you mean to tell me that if Jesus Christ said, 'Thou art Peter, and upon this rock I will build my church . . . ,' you will now refuse to let me have a rock for a marker for my husband's grave. . . ."

Well, a massive salmon-and-beige-colored stone, probably 316 million years old, from the Bistrian quarry, anchors the burial site in Southampton. It's a perfect symbol for what my father loved and stood for.

"Sunset in the West"

Alistair Cooke, in a moving essay entitled "Sunset in the West," in *Letter from America* (BBC Online Network, July 13, 1998), pays tribute, rightly, to the memory of the greatest illusionist/stuntman film has ever known, Yakima Canutt; and at the end of the essay, Mr. Cooke sums up the Gary Cooper image in brilliant fashion:

"For people long familiar both with the West and with the American characters who peopled it as late as sixty years ago, there was Gary Cooper. A man who, for most Americans, during the anxious Hitler days of the thirties, personified the heroic myth of the taut but merciful plainsman who dispenses justice with a worried conscience, a single syllable, a blurred reflex action at the hip, and who faced death in the afternoon as regularly as the matador, but on Main Street, and for no pay.

"Incidentally, no stunt man filled in for him. He was a superb horseman and the best shot Hemingway had ever seen.

"It was in two films, appropriately named *The Plainsman* and *High Noon,* that Cooper best filled this glowing and probably glowingly false picture of the town marshal heading down the railroad tracks back to duty with that precise mince of the cowboy's tread—the rancher's squint that smells mischief in a tumbleweed, sees around corners, and is never fooled.

"Gary Cooper's representation of this hero was not a tough guy necessarily brutal to withstand the brutality of his enemies—he represented every man's secret image of himself: the honorable man slicing through the daily corruption of morals and machines. He isolated and enlarged to six foot three inches an untainted strain of goodness in a very male specimen of the male of the species."

"Gary Cooper was the personification of the honor-bound man."
—Fred Zinnemann

Gary and Veronica, newlyweds, 1933.

Rocky and Gary, 1961. Standing under a big sunflower yellow umbrella in our garden, I took this picture about a month and a half before my father died. We were relaxing around the pool and he was trying to forget the pain that was beginning to dominate his days and nights. But still he managed to enjoy and care about doing whatever little things he *was* able. He was fascinated and delighted when my mother arranged for four black belt judo/karate experts to come over and demonstrate their skills, shattering thick wooden planks, pulverizing three bricks stacked together, with their bare feet. He got totally absorbed in the skill and beauty of it. I could tell he was dying to try it himself, and would have taken lessons if his body had permitted him the strength.

I see this shot and compare it to the early one, where love is new and young, tender and untried. There is great beauty in both, but at the end of the day, the more recent picture is about when two people have weathered life and its travails, its hurdles and pains, its separations and infidelities, and when love wins out over all our human blindness. I think T. S. Eliot captured it exquisitely:

> We shall not cease from exploration
> And the end of all our exploring
> Will be to arrive where we started
> And know the place for the first time.
> —T. S. Eliot, *The Four Quartets*

About two weeks before he died, Poppa asked my mother to bring him a pen and some paper. "I've been trying to remember this," he said. "All that Goddamn pain medicine's made my head not work." He took the paper with a fierce intent, and, indeed, the words did flow from his memory to the page as transcribed below.

Writing it was physically tiring, but he was triumphant when he "got it." They are lines he always loved, from a poem that reflected his own beliefs and actions. The subject of that poem by John Donne came up in our family throughout the years. It wasn't stuck with a magnet on the refrigerator door, but its magnetic force drew us into its orbit, and was a constant in our lives. My mother finished writing the last line.

"No man is an island entire of itself; every man is a piece of the continent, a part of the maine; if a clod be washed away by the Sea, Europe is the lesse, as well as if a promontorie were, as well as if a Manor of thy friends or of thine owne were; any man's death diminishes me, because I am involved in mankind; and therefore never send to know . . . for whom the bell tolls, it tolls for thee."

Epilogue

"My heart knows what the wild goose knows,
and I must go where the wild goose goes."

Once when my father was visiting the Louis Mack ranch near Jackson Hole, Wyoming, two little boys from another ranch heard he was there and made a two-hour pilgrimage on horseback to meet their hero and get his autograph. The Mack family invited them to stay for supper, and when it came time for the boys to go home my father said, "You can't ride all the way home alone, it's getting dark. Cm'on, I'll go with you."

He grabbed a horse and rode with the boys all the way back to their ranch. It didn't matter that it was a four-hour round-trip after sunset—he intended to see that the children got back home safely.

That was Gary Cooper, the man, my father—more than an image on the silver screen, he was a multidimensional, real person—and I hope these pictures from our family albums and the stories in this book have given you a true look at him.

Photograph Credits

Every effort has been made to identify photographers and copyright holders of the material reprinted in this book. The author and publisher gratefully acknowledge the photographers, publications, and individuals listed below who so generously gave their permission and supplied photographs. Those credits not listed in the captions are listed below. References are to page numbers.

Courtesy Slim Aarons, Copyright © Slim Aarons: 87, Copyright © Slim Aarons (Hulton Getty/Liaison): 128–29; AP/Wide World Photo: 12, 15, 85, 91 (below), 92, 139, 147, 148, 150, 154, 155; Courtesy Tillie Arnold, photograph Lloyd R. Arnold: 99, 100, 107 (below), 108 (above and below), 109 (above and below); *Aspen Times:* 52; Baroda Productions, photograph Willard Hatch: 157; Photograph Irving Cantor: 130 (above); Courtesy Cornell Capa, Copyright © Robert Capa: 20 (below), 31, 50, 101, 102, 103, 104–105; Photograph Robert Capa, *Life* magazine © Time Inc.: 114 (above and below); Photograph Coburn © 1940 Samuel Goldwyn: 145; Courtesy Condé Nast, photograph Alexander Paal: 29; Courtesy Mrs. Gary Cooper: 13, 22 (above), 23, 24, 27, 30, 32, 35 (below), 38, 39, 49, 68, 73, 75, 91 (above), 93, 94, 95 (above and below), 96, 107 (above), 120, 122, 130 (below), 133 (below), 134 (below), 137 (above), 144, 170; Courtesy Capa Family, Copyright © Robert Capa: 69 (above); photograph Maria Cooper: 135 (below), 37 (below), 165, 171; photograph Johnny Engstead: 166; photograph Cedric Gibbons: 46; *Look* magazine, photograph Maurice Terrell: 25 (above left); photograph Hal McAlpin: 149 (above); photograph A. L. Whitey Schafer: 48; photograph *Sun Valley News Bureau:* 158; photograph Edward Weston, Copyright © 1981 Center for Creative Photography, Arizona Board of Regents: 47; Photograph Schuyler Crail: 97; *Daily Mirror:* 21; Photograph T. Darvas: 81 (above), 116; Davis Distributing Company: 141; Courtesy David Douglas Duncan, photograph Mrs. Gary Cooper: 115; Copyright © David Douglas Duncan: 117, 118, 119; Photograph G. Felici: 78; Globe Photos: 25 (above right), 169; Goetz-Baroda Productions, photograph Coburn, Jr.: 156; Courtesy Jean Howard, Copyright © Jean Howard: 19, 131 (below), 132 (below), 133 (above), 134 (above), 135 (above); Copyright © George Hurrell: 18; Courtesy Donald Hyatt: 159; Courtesy Maria Cooper Janis: 11, 14, 16; Photograph Yale Joel, *Life* magazine © Time Inc.: 58, 59; *Look* magazine, photograph Maurice Terrell: 33 (left); *Los Angeles Examiner:* 70, 123; Photograph Hal McAlpin: 149 (below); McFadden Publications, photograph Hyman Fink: 90; Photograph Don Ornitz: 153; Courtesy *Paris Match:* 40, 86; photograph Leteuier: 65; photograph Willie Rizzo: 63, 89; photograph Paul Slade: 167 (below); Photograph Bruce Parker: 126, 127; *Photoplay,* photograph Inga Arvad: 33 (right); Courtesy Republic Entertainment, Inc. High Noon © 1952 Republic Entertainment, Inc.: 37; Courtesy RKO Pictures: 20 (above); Sergeant York © 1941 Turner Entertainment Co. All rights reserved: 146; Photograph Peter Stackpole, *Life* magazine © Time Inc.: 35 (above), 56, 57, 74; Photograph Phil Stern: 125; *Sun Valley News Bureau:* 111; *Sun Valley News Service:* 69 (below); Courtesy Roxie Livingston, photograph Earl Theisen: 44, 45, 53, 60, 61, 62, 160, 162, 163; United States Marine Corps: 55; United States Pictures Productions, released through Warner Brothers: 152; Union Pacific Collection: 28; Universal Pictures, a Division of Universal City Studios, Inc. courtesy of MCA Publishing Rights, a Division of MCA Inc.: © 1936, 143; © 1943, 151; Photograph W.: 76.

Acknowledgments

My first thanks are to my mother. If it weren't for her painstaking care throughout the years from 1932 to 1961, in keeping beautiful family albums, this book would not exist. And to my husband, Byron Janis, for all his encouragement and support and . . .

I owe enormous thanks to my agent Robby Lantz. He introduced me to Ruth Peltason of Harry N. Abrams, Inc. She told Paul Gottlieb of the project and happily he okayed it. Ruth has been my most marvelous editor. Her taste and artistic eye and ear brought this book to completion. To the book's designer, Ray Hooper, I extend my deep gratitude.

I could not have done this without the patience and tireless dedication of Sharon Nettles, who took my impossible handwriting into cyberspace and then to the printed page. Her help was invaluable to me.

For my treasured friendship with David Douglas Duncan and his generous contributions to this book, I am eternally grateful. To Slim Aarons, my special thanks for letting "The Kings of Hollywood" be part of this story, and for capturing unique moments. I thank Roxie Theisen Livingston for making available the works of her father, Earl Theisen. Tillie Arnold helped me greatly in identifying and letting me use her husband's marvelous shots of the Cooper-Hemingway days in Sun Valley, Idaho. Lloyd Arnold chronicled a piece of an era and friendship. Special thanks to Mr. Cornell Capa for permitting me to use the marvelous shots made by Robert Capa of our family and the Hemingway adventures. My deep thanks to our longtime friend Jean Howard for permission to use her great and personal photos. I so much appreciate the kindness of Mr. Willie Rizzo in giving me the use of his meaningful pictures.

I'd like to acknowledge Tom Hanks for his introduction, which portrays my father to perfection. To me, Tom Hanks is an actor who embodies the kind of stardom and timeless qualities that I associate with Gary Cooper.

My warmest thanks to Barbara Baker Burrows of *Life* magazine for the extraordinary possibilities her help opened up to me. To Jorge Jaramillo, at AP/Wide World Photos, for his personal kindness and help in letting me research material I could not find elsewhere and to Ray Whelan of Globe Photos, whose vast archives gave me photos I needed, my immense thanks. I want to thank Colette Guerineau and *Paris Match/Scoop Diffusion d'Articles* for all the courtesy they have extended.

I am grateful to the following for giving me permission to use photographs from their archives: AP/Wide World Photos, AP, *Aspen Times*, Davis Distributing Company, Globe Photos, Goetz-Baroda Productions, Goldwyn Productions, *Los Angeles Examiner*, Paramount Pictures, *Paris Match*, Republic Pictures, RKO, Sun Valley Press, Sun Valley News Bureau, Union Pacific Collections, Warner Brothers.

If I have unwittingly omitted thanking anyone, my deep apologies. Many of these photographs from our family albums had no identifying markings at all.

Photographers:

Slim Aarons, Lloyd Arnold, Inga Arvid, Irving Cantor, Robert Capa, Coburn, Coburn, Jr., Schuyler Crail, T. Darvis, David Douglas Duncan, John Engstead, G. Felici, Hyman Fink, Cedric Gibbons, Willard Hatch, Geraldine House, Jean Howard, Hurrell, Donald Hyatt, Yale Joel, John LeRoy Johnston, Leteuier, Hal McAlpin, Robert Morse, Don Ornitz, Alexander Paal, Bruce Parker, Willie Rizzo, Whitey Schafer, Peter Stackpole, Phil Stern, Maurice Terrell, Earl Theisen, Edward Weston

Gary Cooper made this drawing, when he was
only sixteen.